BRICK IN THE LANDSCAPE

Materials in Landscape Architecture and Site Design

Rob W. Sovinski
Brick in the Landscape

BRICK IN THE LANDSCAPE

A Practical Guide to Specification and Design

Rob W. Sovinski, ASLA

JOHN WILEY & SONS, INC.

New York • Chichester • Weinheim • Brisbane • Singapore • Toronto

Copyright © 1999 by John Wiley & Sons, Inc. All rights reserved.

Published simultaneously in Canada.

This publication is designed to provide accurate and authoritative information in regard to the subject matter covered. It is sold with the understanding that the publisher is not engaged in rendering professional services. If professional advice or other expert assistance is required, the services of a competent professional person should be sought.

Library of Congress Cataloging-in-Publication Data:

Sovinski, Rob W.
   Brick in the landscape : a practical guide to specification and
design / Rob W. Sovinski.
        p.   cm.
      Includes bibliographical references and index.
      ISBN 0-471-29358-X (alk. paper)
      1. Bricklaying.   2. Landscape design.   I. Title
   TH5501.S63 1999
   693'.21—dc21   99-14002

To my family

CONTENTS

ACKNOWLEDGMENTS

I would like to thank the following individuals for their valuable contributions to this book: Thomas E. Perry, Director of Marketing, Brick Industry Association; David M. Sovinski, National Director of Market Development and Technical Services, International Masonry Institute; Angie Holt, Pine Hall Brick Co.; Pattie Pandzik, Brickstone Studios; Danielle J. Castello-Weaver, Marketing Services Specialist, Glen-Gery Corporation; Mary Johnson, Endicott Clay Products Co.; Erik "Fuzzy" Gerdes, Computer Specialist, Purdue University. All computer-generated graphics in this text were prepared using Bentley's Microstation and Masterpiece software.

A very special debt of gratitude is owed to Diane Throop, National Director of Technical Services, International Masonry Institute, and Brian Trimble, Director, Technical Services, with the Brick Industry Association, for taking time to review this manuscript in its entirety. Thanks to their valuable input, the reader can be confident that not only is the material presented accurate and reliable, but that it represents current industry recommendations as well.

FOREWORD

Brick is a material for all generations. It is timeless. Yet however timeless it may be, new materials and methods of construction are continually being invented. Keeping up with all of these technological changes is difficult. A book such as *Brick in the Landscape* brings together information from the past and the present to form a continuous legacy.

Brick, with its many colors, textures, patterns, and shapes, offers endless design possibilities. Thoughtful combinations of such properties can result in truly dramatic architecture. Some world-renowned examples: the Colosseum, the Great Wall of China, Jefferson's Monticello, and even Camden Yards ballpark. No other building material offers such a range of choices.

Brick serves a multifunctional purpose in landscapes and architecture. Applications include walls, pavements, columns, piers, retaining walls, screen walls, planters, soffits, beams, barbecues, and mailboxes. Brick not only provides enclosure and aesthetic enhancement, it also serves as structure.

Brick contributes strength, durability, and elegance to projects in which it is used. Although this material has been around for centuries, innovations in its use continue. Prefabricated masonry panels have allowed new methods of construction with masonry, and mortarless systems in pavements and retaining walls have allowed brick to be constructed more economically than in the past.

Brick in the Landscape describes the many attributes of brick in a clear, well-organized format. Landscape architects will finally be able to put their fingers on the many aspects and uses of brick within one publication. I commend Rob Sovinski for presenting so much information within a single source.

Brian E. Trimble
Director, Technical Services
Brick Industry Association, Reston, Virginia

LIST OF ILLUSTRATIONS

1

Pioneer Square in Portland, Oregon. A landscape of brick walls, steps, ramps, pavements and columns.

"Nothing remarkable about a brick, is there? A brick is a brick so far as most people are concerned. And it is not a very beautiful thing, is it? But what you can do with it!"

—FRANK LLOYD WRIGHT

1

INTRODUCTION

As its title suggests, this book deals with brick as both a functional and a design element in the landscape. By *landscape* I mean the human-altered environment. Humans have been in the business of altering the landscape as long as there have been humans. Despite the coming and going of design styles and movements, certain lasting traditions have evolved that typify the way we choose to shape our exterior world. We seek order over chaos, harmony with nature over conflict, and the opportunity for unique cultural or regional expression over global homogeneity. Although "good" design is often difficult to codify precisely, we know it when we see it. Brick is one of a handful of materials that has survived ever-evolving design values and has achieved status as a timeless hallmark of quality in landscape design.

Nature provided humans with their first building materials. Stone, first stacked, then shaped with great difficulty to enhance its capacity for stacking, was undoubtedly among the earliest construction materials used to reshape and reorganize the natural landscape. Where stone was not available, timber or vegetation probably sufficed. But the shaping of stone or wood was a fairly arduous task, given the paucity of tools. We can guess that clay, as a building material, might have been discovered when drought conditions, combined with prolonged exposure to the sun, transformed the usually pliable surface clay deposits into irregularly shaped hardened chips. The ease of shaping the clay while still wet provided a significant advantage. Brick, in some fashion, has been

3

around for millennia and has established itself universally as a timeless landscape tradition. Now, more than ever, there is a clear need on the designer's bookshelf for a manual devoted specifically to the utilization of brick in landscape applications. *Brick in the Landscape* aspires to fill that niche.

Three milestone experiences underscored for me the need for this manual. Much of my professional career was spent working closely with architects, those who were typically trained in the 1950s through the 1970s in the International Style. I vividly recall a meeting that took place in the early 1980s in my office, a large multidisciplinary architectural firm in New York City. The purpose of the meeting to was finalize the selection of the particular brick to be used on a large corporate facility. Present in our boardroom were the project architect, a sales representative from a regional brick supplier, and I. We examined several sample boards that were supplied by the sales representative of a large brick manufacturer. Finally, the architect wagged a finger somewhat menacingly toward one particular sample, admonishing the sales rep that although he was generally satisfied with its color and finish, he would reject any brick delivered to the construction site that varied, even slightly, from the sample provided. Although the sales person did his diplomatic best to explain to the architect about clay and its natural tendencies for variation, the designer stood his ground. A promise by the supplier to "do his absolute best" was tendered, and the project proceeded.

Later I accompanied the architect to the construction site. The installation of the building's exterior brick walls was well under way. The supplier had managed to deliver on his word, and the result was a flat, monochromatic wall, sleek and utterly unwavering in appearance. (Less noticeable was a growing pile of rejected bricks near the project's staging area.) The architect beamed, having accomplished his vision. I, on the other hand, had the uneasy feeling that the same effect could have been achieved using several gallons of reddish-brown paint. The uniform wall lacked any of the richness, interest, or depth of which brick is so capable. I felt as if the brick had somehow been *defeated*—subjugated to perform a task probably better suited to another material or finish.

That same year, I was given the task of planning the site for a large pharmaceutical research facility. Following a few weeks of intense work, I felt confident that my proposal was a well-composed, nicely proportioned design that satisfied the programmatic and functional needs of the facility. With some confidence I presented my drawings to my supervisor. He nodded and agreed that it was a "nice enough design," but he added a challenge: "What about this design will hold the interest of an employee entering the building for the tenth, the fiftieth, or the hundredth time?" He used words like "unfolding" and "layers of meaning." I am not certain I entirely understood his point at the time, but later that year I moved into the London Terrace Apartments in the Chelsea district of New York City. The imposing structure, occupying an entire city block, is a vast and complex composition of brick and carved stone. During the several years I lived there, I never tired of entering that building. Its construction seemed to have called upon every technique and skill known to the masonry trade. My eye picked out some new detail in the relief and the mottled brick of the facade each time I passed by. It was visually captivating, but not cluttered. For me, this building was utterly satisfying, never becoming an invisible element in the background of my daily experience. I never tired of examining its details, its subtle hues, or its massing. I began to understand my supervisor's point.

I recently attended the national convention of the American Society of Landscape Architects. A typical fixture at these conventions is the familiar display area where vendors tout their products, often with special emphasis on the latest innovations. This year was no exception. It seemed as if there were acres of display booths, each occupied by well-mannered and well-dressed representatives. I was struck by the number of products that, although not *exactly* brick, sought to emulate brick and capitalize on its universal appeal. One booth promoted a process that enabled one to convincingly stamp a brick pattern into wet concrete; pattern, texture, and even color could be controlled to simulate brick. But it *was not* brick. And its appearance, although nice enough, did not simulate brick to a degree that anyone would suspect it of being anything but concrete. Elsewhere, a number of booths were promoting products that *resembled* bricks but were actually composed of precast concrete. They were available in a wide variety of shapes and colors and could be assembled in a number of unique patterns. In truth, many were very handsome products. Colorful photographs displayed an appealing array of options for patios and drives. Yet I could not avoid the feeling that this was some kind of sleight-of-hand. The ad slogan "Just as good as a Xerox" came to mind. A bit less palatable was a product that created a stenciled brick pattern over wet concrete, achieved after a color hardener was broadcast over the surface. When the stencil was removed, the result was a sort of two-dimensional brick pattern. The idea behind each of these products is respectable enough, and *Brick in the Landscape* in no way aspires to serve as a treatise for material elitism. These comments should be taken as observations more than criticisms. Time alone will tell whether we will embrace or reject faux building materials. Their presence at trade shows and in advertisements suggests that some degree of acceptance has already occurred. But, as with most attempts to copy a more authentic original, the effect is only skin deep and nobody is *really* being fooled.

The philosophies and design theories of Frank Lloyd Wright offer a refreshing philosophical perspective for designers. Wright's genius was guided by a set of more or less codified design principles. In particular, his essay "The Nature of Materials" is a call for celebrating a material's authenticity and its relationship to the landscape. His buildings and furnishings reflect that passion for authenticity. His palette was simple and eschewed artifice and the synthetic. Wood, stone, glass, copper, and, of course, brick were among his favorite materials. The result was a sublime relationship between architecture and nature.

The beauty inherent in brick results not only from the skills and attention of the manufacturer and the judgment and craftsmanship of the mason; it derives from the accumulated knowledge and talent of the designer as well. The talented landscape designer who also possesses skill in detailing is best poised to utilize brick to its fullest potential. The mission of *Brick in the Landscape* is to provide that knowledge, to place between the covers of a single text, concisely and conveniently within the designer's reach, the information needed to skillfully undertake landscape design with brick.

This book seeks not only to assist landscape designers with technical information but to provide an inspirational source for ideation as well. In one

Frank Lloyd Wright's J. H. Amberg House, Grand Rapids, Michigan. Wright employed the horizontality of brick to marry building and site into a harmonious whole.

form or another, brick remains among the most widely used construction materials on the planet. Its legacy of use in the human-made environment, both in our buildings and in our landscapes, deserves our continued consideration as a rich, versatile, and durable construction unit.

Brick in the Landscape is a technical reference manual intended to aid in the design process. As such, it is meant for use by anyone who seeks to achieve quality masonry design and installation in the built landscape. Certainly professionals such as landscape architects, architects, and landscape designers will find it useful, but the do-it-yourself home owner who is looking for a clear and concise resource on garden masonry will appreciate its straightforward approach as well.

Here, both new and extant information is combined in a single, convenient reference for any individual engaged in landscape design. Given its long tradition and history, the subject of brick is inevitably encountered by historic preservationists and advocates. A unique aspect of this book is its reintroduction of some all-but-forgotten methods and techniques that had been used by masons and bricklayers for centuries. Can you skintle, diaper, or corbel? The text features these and other time-honored techniques.

The material found between the covers of *Brick in the Landscape* will not teach you how to manufacture your own bricks, nor will it prepare you for a career as a bricklayer. The training and apprenticeship required of today's masons goes well beyond the scope of this text. However, landscape architects, landscape designers, and most experienced do-it-yourselfers will find this manual helpful and informative. It penetrates the surface and seeks to reveal more clearly the techniques that result in quality design, detailing, and installation of brick in the landscape.

Finally, *Brick in the Landscape* is two books in one. Professional landscape designers and landscape architects who are using this book as a resource are probably in the midst of one or more projects, each with pressing deadlines. The time required to read anything, let alone an entire book, is precious and scarce. At the end of each section in Chapters 3, 4, and 5, readers will find a brief summary entitled "The Busy Designer's Quick Reference Guide." This guide features the key points made in each section. Depth and background are vitally important in gaining a thorough working knowledge of brick and its uses, but sometimes designers need information quickly and given simply. Busy designers will also find the appendices at the end of this book useful and succinct. These include a guide for metric conversion standards for masonry, a listing of technical support resources, and a glossary of brick terms.

2

The richness and warmth of brick adds to the intimacy of private gardens.

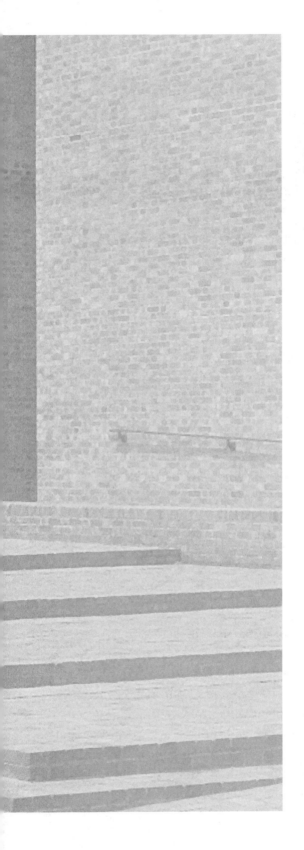

2

THE TRADITION OF BRICK

WHY BRICK?

AUTHENTICITY

Brick is the real thing. It is fired earth, a process that does not begin in a kiln but, rather, results from the formation of shales and clays over geologic time spans. Brick offers rich red to brown to tan hues that are not the result of artificial dyes or admixtures, but are organic expressions of the variable regional soil deposits from which it is composed. Its presence in the built landscape appears graceful, appropriate, and authentic. A brick surface is mottled and warm. It begins as a beautiful crafted artifact and ages gracefully, taking on the rich patina of time and weathering. Brick is a human-scaled material that is wonderfully suited to the environments we construct. Its general size and proportions have evolved from its ability to fit neatly into a worker's hand, a trait that makes it ideal for craftsworkers and craftsmanship. Brick neither overwhelms nor disappears in the landscape, but rather holds its place and serves its purpose with dignity and strength. Frank Lloyd Wright wrote and spoke often of the importance of the authenticity of the construction materials that composed his buildings. Wright's designs celebrate the nature, capacity, and spirit of

11

Bethesda Fountain, New York City. The centerpiece of Olmsted's Central Park features a broad, brick-paved plaza.

the materials from which they are constructed. It is difficult to find artifice or simulation in his designs. Frequently, brick was his material of choice. His buildings and homes utilized brick masonry as an effective tool with which to marry building and site, a means of integrating structure and beauty. Brick is *of the earth,* but *shaped by humans.* Its application in the landscape evokes a powerful sense of place and the spirit of a region.

QUALITY

Brick carries with it a reputation of distinction. Because of their *perceived* economies, the physical landscape in which we live features an expanding quantity of asphalt, concrete, and, increasingly, synthetic building materials. While these materials compose the background of our built environment, brick provides a delightful counterpoint within this context and suggests a heightened concern for quality, beauty, and durability. Used in the landscape, brick signifies a commitment to quality. A well-designed and installed brick wall or pavement is not the result of cutting and pasting the same tired detail into blueprints, but rather the results of thoughtful detailing and learned craftsmanship.

This brick walk suggests elegance, dignity, and history.

Well-detailed masonry puts on public display the skills of the installer and the designer. (Courtesy of Pine Hall Brick Company.)

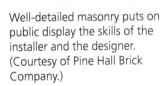

Brick has the remarkable capacity to serve ever-evolving styles and periods.

HISTORY

The history of brick spans thousands of years. To use brick is to build on its time-honored tradition of masonry craftsmanship. Each new landscape that humans build on our planet grows out of a tradition of past parks, towns, plazas, gardens, and open spaces. Brick establishes the connection to the past vividly and clearly. Brick speaks of who we are, but also of who we were. Yet although brick pays sincere homage to our history, it is not narrowly defined as a "historical" material; that is, it does not belong solely to a particular period in history. A testament to its timelessness is the fact that that brick has remained in favor despite the passing of countless stylistic movements. Both the romantic baroque and the severely modern embraced brick as a material aptly capable of expressing their unique tenets.

FLEXIBILITY

There are no rigid formulas for designing with brick. Given its relatively small unit size and its range of available colors, surfaces, and finishes, the potential for innovation is limited only by the knowledge and skill of the designer. The designer who is empowered with a working knowledge of brick patterns, bonds, surface arrangements, and technical capabilities has at hand a virtually unlimited creative palette. That designer is poised to achieve the depth of surface, relief, plasticity, shadowing, variegation, and unique visual qualities of which brick is capable.

The relatively small unit size of brick enables, rather than restricts, the creative designer.

WHEN IS A BRICK A BRICK?

Seemingly a simple concept, "brick" turns out to be a surprisingly slippery term. Like the meaning of "all natural," the definition of *brick* depends on the speaker. A typical dictionary definition of brick describes a molded, rectangular block of clay baked by the sun or fired in a kiln until hard and used as a building and paving material. Common usage has expanded this definition to include almost any building material that *resembles* brick in color or shape.

Brick is fired clay or pulverized shale. It results from the mining, reshaping, and firing of a particular type of the earth's soil. The unique molecular quality of clay ideally lends itself to an easily molded and extremely durable building material. The color of brick results from its mineral content and the presence of metallic oxides. Its variability from source to source results in a range of hues and tones rather than uniformity. Throughout this book, the term *brick* will refer exclusively to oven-fired earth building units. Without meaning to criticize their use in landscape applications, this text will not discuss precast or cast-in-place concrete masonry units. Nor will it investigate asphalt pavers, although they are available in dimensions similar to those of brick. Some may argue that the term *brick* technically refers to the size alone of the masonry unit, regardless of its composition. To avoid confusion among designers and their clients, I prefer to define any brick-sized masonry unit made from formed concrete as a *concrete masonry unit* (CMU), a *concrete paver,* or, at best, a *concrete brick,* although the first term is normally reserved for the description of concrete blocks. Likewise, brick-shaped asphalt units should be categorized as *asphalt block pavers.* None of these contains clay, nor are they kiln fired or baked in the sun to achieve their final strength. The bricklike color range of concrete pavers is achieved through the addition of pigments in their sand, aggregate, water, and cement mix. Among the primary selling points of alternative brick-shaped units is their uniformity in size and ease of manufacturing. In truth, size, color, and finish may be controlled to a somewhat greater degree during the manufacture of precast products than in the manufacture of true bricks. To some designers, however, the single biggest drawback of many bricklike substitutes is that self-same unvariegated uniformity.

Another building material often closely associated with brick is terracotta. The name comes from the Latin *terra cocta,* which literally translated means "baked earth." But that would apply to our definition of brick as well. What, then, differentiates brick from terra-cotta? One difference is that the clay used in terra-cotta is more refined. It contains fewer impurities and is finer grained than the clay used in brick production. Because of its enhanced workability, terra-cotta lends itself extremely well to the manufacture of detailed architectural ornamentation. Although not absolutely essential to the definition of terra-cotta, this historical use as ornamentation is perhaps what first comes to mind when distinguishing between terra-cotta and brick.

For landscape designers, the decision to use brick entails a tremendous range of choices and options. How durable must it be? How impervious to water penetration? What color range best suits the project? What dimensions and/or shapes of brick are appropriate? What surface treatment (finish) should be used? How shall the bricks be bonded together? The variations within these and other options, the source and composition of raw materials, and the varied methods of manufacturing brick result in a virtually unlimited palette of choices for the designer.

Brick adapted to a diversity of uses in the built environment.

A BRIEF HISTORY OF BRICK AND BRICK MAKING

This book is intended to serve designers, facilitating their use of brick in landscape applications. Toward that goal, I have endeavored to keep it concise and compact. Yet no design curriculum can be considered complete without the study of that field's unique history, and no designers should consider themselves adequately prepared without a working knowledge of that history. Composer and musician Benjamin Verdery once explained to a student why a knowledge of J. S. Bach was a critical step in becoming a complete musician. "By playing Bach's music we have a direct relationship to one of the greatest musical minds in Western civilization." And so may we establish a direct link to the master builders of the past when we design with masonry. Although creativity is a key component, the process of design is not a purely inventive endeavor. It draws on the deep traditions established by every master mason, designer, gardener, architect, and landscape architect who came before us. An understanding of a material's past and its traditions are just as essential for the composition of skillful and meaningful designs as a knowledge of their current properties and requirements.

A decorative molded brick from the eighteenth century.

Certainly the use of stone as a building material predates brick by a wide margin. The practice of gathering stone and ultimately shaping it with ever increasing precision is doubtless as old as humankind. Whereas stone is a *raw material,* however, brick is a *manufactured material.* The process of sun drying and later kiln firing hand-shaped clay building units can now be reliably dated back approximately 10,000 years. Brick, then, is the oldest manufactured building material. It is widely held that the first evidence of brick can be traced to Jericho, circa 8,000 B.C. The earliest bricks were rounded, oblong-shaped units resembling loaves of bread. Their lack of sharp, right-angled corners facilitated curved architectural forms. They were sized to fit neatly into the worker's grasp, an attribute that continues to distinguish brick today. The early bricks were shaped by hand and baked in the sun. Given the tendency of sunbaked mud to shrink unpredictably and break easily, early brick makers introduced straw into the clay, along with other available organic materials such as dung and, later, sand into the mix. Despite the impressive technological advances that will continue to distance contemporary manufacturing from its earliest incarnation, brick remains essentially unchanged. It is, as it was, fired earth shaped into a more or less standardized set of dimensions. Only a handful of significant technical innovations mark the advance of brick over the millennia. Between 3000 B.C. and 2500 B.C. the Mesopotamians provided the single greatest step forward in brick technology by baking bricks in kilns. Kiln-fired bricks were significantly harder and more durable than those left in the sun to bake. As a building material, kiln-fired brick rivaled stone, whose quarrying and shaping were time-consuming and labor-intensive. It was also during this approximate time period that brick began to be molded in wood forms rather than hand shaped, yielding a more standardized and consistent building unit.

By 2000 B.C. there is clear evidence that the Chinese had begun to build with sun-dried brick. Eventually, the Chinese would take full advantage of the high strength achieved by the kiln-firing of brick in the construction of the Great Wall. Knowledge of brick manufacturing technology spread roughly along trade routes or was acquired among the spoils of war. It was the Romans' conquest of the Etruscans that, in all likelihood, provided them with the technology necessary to skillfully craft kiln-fired bricks. Like the Greeks before them, they produced high-quality fired bricks, but held a low opinion of brick as a decorative material. Economical and widely available, brick was typically regarded for its strength, but was usually concealed beneath a thick layer of an applied finish, such as plaster. Not until the Middle Ages was brick aggressively and widely exploited for its decorative potential. A rich tradition of graceful and intricate brickwork arose throughout Europe. With this expertise firmly established in England, France, Holland, and Spain, brick manufacturing technologies and design traditions were natural exports to the New World. Colonized communities found brick an affordable, available, secure, and fire-resistant building material from the outset. Postrevolutionary America's first great architect, Thomas Jefferson, made brick an essential component of his home, Monticello, and in both buildings and landscape elements at the University of Virginia. Brick became a simple, honest expression of the young democracy.

Brick has become an iconic element of America's colonial period landscapes.

The simple, honest dignity of brick was appropriate for the young democracy.

So indelible is the mark brick made on early North American colonial architecture, that the use of brick in architecture and landscape design is seen as an essential part of early American landscapes.

Frank Lloyd Wright, endeavoring to establish a "truly American architecture," relied heavily on brick as an essential element both in his early Prairie-style design tenets and later in the homes of his Usonian period. Wright can be credited with popularizing the more horizontally proportioned Roman-size brick, as he used it to further emphasize the horizontality of his innovative architecture.

A Usonian house by Frank Lloyd Wright. An expression of horizontality fitting for an American landscape.

The modern period of architecture, while eschewing "needless" decoration and ornament, promoted a smoother, machinelike design aesthetic. Designers pushed for a more consistent color range with less variation, a trait not always integral to the manufacture of brick. At its best, the modern movement yielded bold, simple compositions that approached the qualities of pure sculpture. Brick, so capable of creating surface depth, relief, pattern and interest was typically configured into flat, unbroken panels using simple bond patterns. Traditional and historical methods and techniques made their way into architects' blueprints with less and less frequency, and a great deal of knowledge and craftsmanship was either lost or set aside. It is unfortunate that the postmodern period, which now seeks to acknowledge a historical debt, lacks a solid, well-established tradition of craftsmanship in detailing with brick.

An unfortunate result of the frequent misinterpretation of the tenets of the modern movement was the rush to develop cheaper and, sadly, less durable building materials, and their widespread adoption as acceptable architectural paradigms. Brick emerged from this period as a high-end construction material, an ironic turnabout considering its humble past. Shunned

A brick landscape from the modern era. Clean, simple lines and a monochromatic palette were among the hallmarks of modernism.

by the Greeks and, later, the Romans as being too crude for finished architectural design, brick is now often perceived by consumers and touted by builders as a costly, nearly luxurious option. This trend, in turn, has given rise to a myriad of increasingly synthetic alternative building materials. It is telling that many of these "economical" choices go to great lengths to appear "bricklike." Although essentially artificial, these materials and processes are too often perceived by designers as acceptable alternatives to authentic brick.

Today's brick might appear foreign to those whose hands first shaped mud and left it in the sun to dry some 10,000 years ago, buts its ancestry is undeniable. The history of brick and its technological advances dovetail with the history of building and design. Intertwined with its evolution was the need for individuals skilled and knowledgeable in its limitless potential and its unique requirements. As Benjamin Verdery advised his student, only by knowing the past may you take your place in an unbroken line spanning centuries of craftsmanship, knowledge, artistry, and technique.

3

Exterior brickwork must be capable of withstanding an enormous range of human and environmental stresses. (Courtesy of Glen-Gery Corporation. Photograph by Tim Schoon, York, Pennsylvania.)

3
MATERIALS AND PROPERTIES

CLAY AND SHALE: THE RAW MATERIALS OF BRICK

The earth's soil is generally classified in three broad categories: sand, silt, and clay. Of these, clay has the greatest plasticity and workability. These qualities, combined with its availability over many regions, has led humans to shape both useful and beautiful artifacts from clay for more than 10,000 years. Because clay is a naturally occurring material, its content varies widely, producing distinct regional variations in the resulting bricks. Clay, in its purest state, is composed mainly of silica and alumina. The specific mineral content of clay, along with its impurities, affects the color and structural characteristics of the finished brick. For the manufacture of brick, clay is divided into two categories, calcareous (containing calcium carbonate) and noncalcareous. Calcareous clays fire to a yellowish color, and noncalcareous clays yield brick in the reddish range. Owing to the relative ease of access, clay found near the surface has been used longest for brick production. Surface clays typically contain a greater amount of oxides than deeper clays, which reduces their tolerance to high temperatures.

Shale is a sedimentary material composed of compacted clay deposits. Although costlier to extract than clay, shale is also used in brick making. Shale must first undergo a process in which it is pulverized. During this process the shale is essentially transformed again into its parent clay material.

Fire clays are found deeper in the earth and are composed of a very pure form of clay containing fewer oxides than surface clays. Fire clays are well suited to the manufacture of brick that will be exposed to high levels of heat, such as in fireplaces and flues.

THE BUSY DESIGNER'S QUICK REFERENCE GUIDE:
Methods of Brick Production

- Clay is composed primarily of silica and alumina.
- Calcareous clays yield yellowish bricks.
- Noncalcareous clays yield reddish bricks.
- Shale must be pulverized for use in brick production.
- Deeper clays are finer and yield bricks that tolerate higher temperatures than surface clays.

METHODS OF BRICK PRODUCTION

The initial step in manufacturing brick is the mining of the clay. Once extracted from the pit, clay must be prepared prior to shaping and firing. The clay is then ground into a fine powder, ready to be mixed with water for forming. Bricks are typically formed by one of three methods:

Soft-mud process (molded)

Stiff-mud process (extrusion)

Dry-press process

The *soft-mud process,* the oldest method of forming brick, is so named because it introduces the highest volume of water into the ground clay prior to forming. The "muddy" wet clay mix is placed in an open-topped mold. Excess clay is scraped from the top of the mold. Two methods for facilitating removal of the clay from the form are the water-struck and the sand-struck processes. Water-striking yields a smoother face to the brick, while the more commonly used sand-struck method yields bricks with a grittier surface.

The *stiff-mud process* is the most prevalent method used to produce bricks today. During this process only enough water is added for the clay to stick together (about half the amount used in the soft-mud process.) By extruding the clay through a die shaped to the desired width and length of the brick, a long ribbon of clay is produced. The clay is finally cut by wires to the specified height. Manufacturers have a wide range of texturing attachments and surface treatments that may be used as the smooth brick is extruded. Any necessary coring may also take place during the extrusion. The long column of continuous clay is cut by wire into individual units. The method is well adapted to assembly line processes and permits the production of a high volume of consistent bricks.

The third method of forming bricks is the *dry-press process*. A clay of very low plasticity works best in this method. Dry-pressing uses even less water than the stiff-mud process, relying on high pressure to produce a brick that is very dense and consistent in shape and dimension. The water content of the clay is less than 10%. The clay is shaped in steel molds, where pressure between 500 and 1,500 psi is applied, resulting in very precisely shaped clay units. The dry-press method accounts for only a small percentage of bricks currently produced in the United States.

Each of these methods produces unfired, or "green," bricks. Green bricks are either air-dried or, now more commonly, kiln-dried prior to firing to further reduce their moisture content. Once dried, the green bricks are fired in a kiln. Much of the strength and weather resistance of a particular brick results from its firing. Since the earliest times when shaped mud was first laid in the sun to bake into a hardened building unit, the technology of baking and then firing has been the subject of continuous technological research and advancement. Today, computer monitored and operated tunnel kilns provide manufacturers with a great deal of precision in controlling the firing process. Each individual brick receives carefully regulated and consistent exposure to the heat, a condition not possible with older methods whereby stationary brick was stacked in a periodic or beehive kiln for firing. Initially, the bricks are heated at relatively low temperatures to remove moisture. The firing of brick then requires a gradual increasing of the kiln's temperature and may take as much as 50 hours of firing in a tunnel kiln. Partial vitrification, the ceramic fusing of the clay that gives brick its strength, durability, and water resistance, takes place at temperatures ranging up to 2100°F (1149°C).

THE BUSY DESIGNER'S QUICK REFERENCE GUIDE:
Methods of Brick Production

- The three methods of brick production are the soft-mud process, the stiff-mud process, and the dry-press method.
- Bricks are molded to shape in the soft-mud process and the dry-press method.
- Bricks are shaped by extrusion during the stiff-mud process.
- The stiff-mud process accounts for most of the brick in use today.
- Molded bricks may be water-struck or sand-struck.
- During firing, green brick is partially vitrified, which produces its weather resistance and durability.
- Modern kilns are called "tunnel kilns."
- Bricks are fired in kilns at temperatures up to 2100°F (1149°C).

CLASSIFICATION OF BRICK

The various methods of grading and classifying brick often proves to be a confusing topic for designers. Simply put, brick is classified according to its intended use and function. For vertical applications, brick is classified in two broad categories, building (or common) brick and facing brick.

WEATHERING

The forces of nature work incessantly to degrade most human constructs, and brick is certainly not exempt. The American Society for Testing and Materials (ASTM) has established three weathering zones in the United States. Brick recommended for areas subject to severe weathering dynamics is designated as grade SW, for severe weathering. SW bricks are manufactured to resist frequent exposure to water and the forces of freezing and thawing cycles. Grade SW is therefore the best candidate for below-grade masonry installations as well, even in geographic zones not designated SW. Grade MW (moderate weathering) brick has less resistance to moisture and freezing and is recommended for above-grade use in moderate weathering zones. Grade NW (negligible weathering) is not recommended for landscape applications.

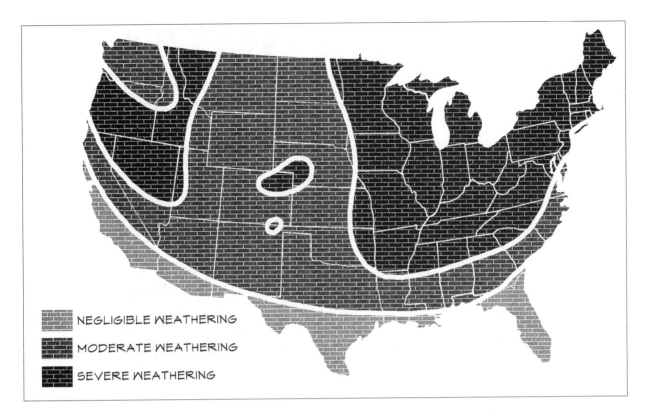

NEGLIGIBLE WEATHERING

MODERATE WEATHERING

SEVERE WEATHERING

Given the relatively insignificant difference in cost, the unpredictability of climate, and a desire for greater durability, it is hard to justify the use of anything other than grade SW.

Zones of relative weather severity in the United States.

FACING BRICK

Facing brick is the workhorse of the brick palette. As its name suggests, facing brick features at least one face intended to be visible in the finished construction. The ASTM specification for facing brick permits the designer to call for a particular finish, texture, and color. So-called solid facing brick is covered under ASTM C216, Standard Specification for Facing Brick, which designates three types, FBS (facing brick, standard), FBX (facing brick, select), and FBA (facing brick, architectural). Confusion often arises when a specified solid unit arrives at the job site riddled with core holes. ASTM permits manufacturers to designate a brick as "solid" provided the holes do not exceed 25% of its bearing surface area. Designers should take care to order the necessary quantity of *non-cored* bricks whose shiner surface is exposed. Few details detract from an otherwise well-designed landscape as much as exposed core holes.

Exposed core holes detract from an otherwise skillful design.

According to ASTM C216, Type FBS brick is intended for general masonry use. The specification for Type FBX calls for higher levels of precision where consistency in each brick's overall size and dimension is needed. Type FBA brick is manufactured for specific, nonuniform architectural effects in its size, color finish, or texture.

Facing brick is categorized according to Grades SW and MW. Designers should note that when they fail to specify a brick's grade or type, Grade SW and Type FBS are the default classifications.

HOLLOW FACING BRICK

An alternative to solid brick is hollow facing brick. Hollow units are finding increasing use, gaining ground against traditional solid bricks. These are governed by ASTM C652 and are defined as bricks whose holes or voids exceed 25% of the bearing surface area. ASTM discusses four categories of hollow brick, HBS, HBX, HBA, and HBB. When not specified, HBS is the default standard. The S, X, and A suffixes parallel those for facing brick very closely. HBB designates a hollow brick whose finish, color, and precise dimensions are not of concern to the designer.

BUILDING BRICK

A brief discussion of building brick, governed by ASTM C62, is included here as a necessary part of the overall range of available brick materials. Landscape designers, however, will probably find little use for building brick. Even in architectural detailing, where it was traditionally used as an unseen backup material, building brick is used much less frequently today. Increasingly fewer specifications call for this material.

PEDESTRIAN AND LIGHT-TRAFFIC PAVING BRICK

Because of its more vulnerable exposure to weathering and the constant stress of traffic, even light-traffic paving brick must maintain higher compressive strength and lower porosity than either building or facing brick. ASTM C902 establishes the criteria for pedestrian and light-traffic paving brick. ("Light-

A rich and serviceable brick pavement intended for pedestrian and light vehicular traffic. (Courtesy of Glen-Gery Corporation. Photograph by Tim Schoon, York, Pennsylvania.)

traffic" refers to pavements that receive limited vehicular traffic at low speeds, such as driveways.) ASTM C1272 deals with heavy-use vehicular pavers, and is discussed in the following paragraph. The classification of light traffic paving brick is dependent on its intended application and use. There are three weathering *classes* of paving brick, and three *types,* based on anticipated traffic and required levels of resistance to abrasion by traffic.

Classes of Light-Traffic Paving Brick

Class SX (severe exposure) should be specified where pavements may encounter freezing while saturated with water. In contrast to building and facing bricks, Class SX paving bricks must maintain a minimum average compressive strength of 8,000 psi, and an individual unit cannot have a strength below 7,000 psi. Class MX (moderate exposure) may be called for in southern climates where freezing is not expected, and Class NX (negligible exposure) is intended for interior use only and should not be considered by landscape designers.

Types of Light-Traffic Paving Brick

Type I bricks are recommended where highly abrasive traffic is anticipated, such as in driveways or heavily concentrated pedestrian zones. Type II bricks are best suited for typical pedestrian environments such as public walkways. Type III bricks offer the least resistance to abrasion and should be used in low-traffic residential applications.

HEAVY VEHICULAR PAVING BRICK

Where vehicular traffic is greater in speed, volume, and weight, a stronger brick is naturally required. Brick in heavy traffic situations must not only tolerate the added structural load, but are subjected to greater abrasion and the tendency for both horizontal and twisting forces as well. This material is governed by ASTM C1272, Standard Specification for Heavy Vehicular Paving Brick.

Classification of Heavy Vehicular Paving Brick

The American Society for Testing and Materials has established two *types* and three *application classifications* for heavy vehicular paving brick. Type R paving brick is intended for situations where a rigid or semirigid setting bed and base are provided, such as concrete or asphalt. With Type R pavers, the minimum average compressive strength is set at 8,000 psi, with the rigid setting bed and base contributing to the overall compressive strength of the profile. Type R pavers carry a minimum thickness dimension of 2¼ in. Conversely, Type F brick is a stronger brick, better suited for use with a flexible setting or leveling bed, such as sand or stone screenings, along with an adequately compacted base material. Type F pavers are required to achieve a higher overall compressive strength than type R pavers, with a minimum average of 10,000 psi. Type F pavers must maintain a thickness of no less than 2⅝ in.

ASTM C1272 also identifies three application classifications for standard, extra, and architectural purposes. Application classification PS refers to heavy paving brick for general, all-purpose use. Where there is greater concern for overall uniformity, including precision of dimension, degree of warping, and chipping, designers should specify application PX. Application PA deals with paving bricks whose specific visual characteristics, such as size, color, and texture, are more closely controlled.

CLINKER BRICK

Clinker bricks are irregularly shaped bricks that are valued by designers for their texture, character, low porosity, and hardness. They are often specified by designers seeking to impart a historical look or feel to a project. Clinker bricks are the result of an older firing technology, whereby bricks were stacked vertically in a coal-fired beehive kiln. Because of the inherent uneven distribution of heat, the bricks on the bottom of the stack were fired to a harder state than those above. This prolonged exposure to the hottest zone of the kiln frequently resulted in clinkers—misshaped, warped, or twisted bricks—which were typically sorted. Those considered unusable were culled. Modern tunnel kilns have eliminated uneven heat distribution, along with the resulting clinker bricks. Still, they remain available from a number of sources utilizing older kilns for the express purpose of producing these unusual and charming bricks. The sorting of usable clinker bricks tends to push the cost higher than tunnel-kiln-fired bricks. Extremely deformed clinker bricks can be difficult to lay and require abnormally wide mortar joints in order to maintain level courses.

BRICK SIZES

MODULARITY IN BRICK MASONRY

For efficiency in production, design, and construction, a set of standardized modular dimensions has evolved for many facets of the building industry. Brick masonry is no exception. In 1962, John Wiley & Sons published *Modular Practice,* establishing a 4 in. modular grid for laying brick. The photograph below shows the alignment of the four inch modular grid relative to mortar joints. Minor irregularities or differences in the actual dimensions of the brick are accommodated in the joint. So long as the 4 in. rule is adhered to, the masonry construction will remain modular. Modularity in brick masonry is tremendously useful to designers, permitting them to develop precise coursing and bonding details with confidence.

Eight-in. (nominal) concrete block is often used as a backup material for vertical brick surfaces, so it is critical that block and brick are sized to coincide at regular intervals. Modular brick is sized so that the brick joints align at either every 8 in. or every 16 in. interval of typical concrete block coursing. Using 4 in. concrete blocks, commonly known as "half-highs," reduces the coursing necessary for alignment but increases the number of concrete masonry units (CMUs) that must be handled. This alignment facilitates tying the brick to the block via mechanical ties or with a header. It also ensures that the topmost courses of brick and block will align, minimizing the cutting of units. It should be noted that block of this dimension is not nearly as available as standard 8 in. units and may be difficult to obtain in some areas.

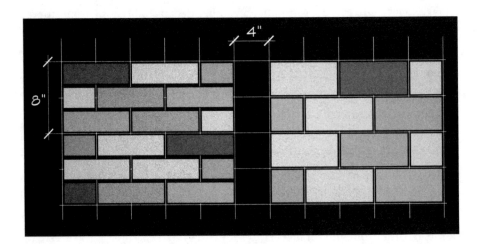

Modularity in brickwork is based on 4 in. multiples of its nominal sizes.

THE BUSY DESIGNER'S QUICK REFERENCE GUIDE:
Classification of Brick

The ASTM refers to the American Society for Testing and Materials (ASTM) establishes and publishes approved guides, practices, and test methods for brick and other construction materials

- "Weathering" is a measure of a brick's ability to withstand exposure to the elements.

- Classification SW stands for *severe* weathering, MW stands for *moderate* weathering, and NW refers to *negligible* weathering.

- Facing brick is the brick most commonly specified. Building brick is infrequently specified.

- The three types of facing brick are FBS (facing brick, standard), FBX (facing brick, select), and FBA (facing brick, architectural).

- A brick may be designated as "solid," provided the holes do not exceed 25% of its bearing surface area.

- Hollow facing brick has voids that exceed 25% of its bearing surface area.

- Hollow facing brick is categorized as HBS (hollow brick, standard), HBX (hollow brick, select), HBA (hollow brick, architectural), and HBB (hollow brick for general use).

- Light-traffic paving brick is intended for pedestrian pavements or vehicular pavements that receive limited traffic at low speeds, such as driveways.

- The three *classes* of light-traffic paving brick are SX paving bricks, (severe exposure), MX (moderate exposure), and Class NX (negligible exposure, for interior use).

- The three *types* of light-traffic paving bricks are Type I (for highly abrasive traffic areas), Type II (for typical pedestrian environments), and Type III (for low-traffic residential applications).

- Heavy vehicular paving brick is intended for use where vehicular traffic is greater in speed, volume, and weight.

- The three *classifications* of heavy vehicular paving brick are PS (general, all-purpose use), PX (better overall uniformity), and PA (for specific visual characteristics).

- The two *types* of heavy vehicular paving brick are Type R, where a rigid or a semirigid setting bed and base are provided, and Type F, a stronger brick better suited for use with a flexible setting bed.

- Clinker bricks are irregularly shaped bricks that achieve a harder state owing to their location in a beehive kiln.

STANDARDIZATION OF BRICK DIMENSIONS

Historically, brick tended to be manufactured and constructed locally. Local and regional differences in sizes and nomenclature created problems for designers and specifiers. Today, 90% of all manufactured brick adheres to a set of established standards that govern the size and nomenclature of modular and nonmodular brick units. This standardization facilitates the design process, ensuring that the proposed configuration can be installed and that the desired brick units are available. Builders and contractors also benefit from the simplicity of estimating the quantity of standardized bricks required for a particular job and being able to source the project competitively from a larger number of suppliers. In specifying brick, dimensions are listed in a standardized sequence. *Width* is designated first, followed by *height,* and the *length.* Length and height relate to the exposed face of a brick laid as a stretcher and are often referred to as its face dimensions. In a stretcher configuration, the width is the dimension of the brick that penetrates into the wall.

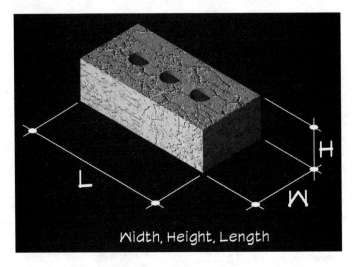

Width, Height, Length

The standard designation of a brick's nominal or specified dimensions is given in width, height, and length.

NOMINAL VERSUS ACTUAL DIMENSIONS

Anyone familiar with basic construction is aware that the common two-by-four piece of lumber is not actually 2 in. by 4 in. in section. "Two-by four" is a *nominal* (in name only) designation. The *actual* dimensions are somewhat less. Like lumber, modular brick differs in actual size from its nominal

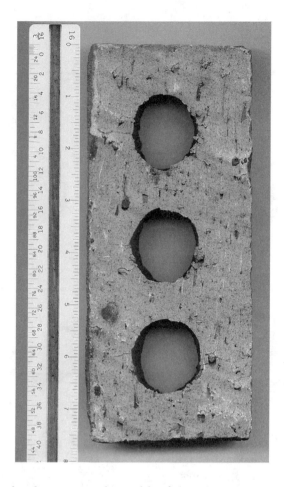

Modular brick has three sets of dimensions. The nominal length of this brick is 8 in. Its specified length is 7⅝ in., and its actual length measures 7¹¹⁄₁₆ in.

dimensions. In brick masonry, the width of the mortar joint accounts for the difference. The nominal dimension of a brick equals the sum of the actual dimension plus the width of one mortar joint. Using nominal rather than actual sizes is critical in estimating the number of bricks that will be required for a particular job.

ACTUAL VERSUS SPECIFIED DIMENSIONS

In addition to *nominal* and *actual* dimensions, a third designation, *specified* dimension, is important to understand. The specified dimension is the size of the brick as it is *intended* to be manufactured. Such dimensions should be included in the project specifications. The specified dimensions should not be confused with the actual dimensions. For a variety of reasons, related to raw material and to processing, the actual dimensions of bricks will vary from one to another. ASTM standards require actual dimensions to fall within an acceptable range. Specifiers should refer to ASTM C216, Standard Specification for Facing Brick, for acceptable tolerances. Nominal and specified dimensions of the most common standard modular and nonmodular sizes are shown on the following page. See also Table 3.1.

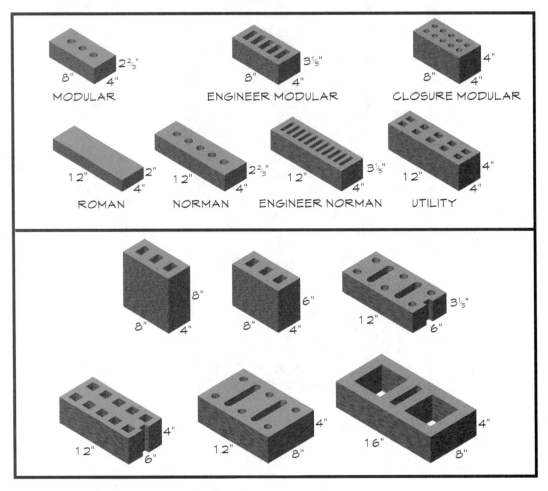

Modular brick sizes with nominal dimensions.

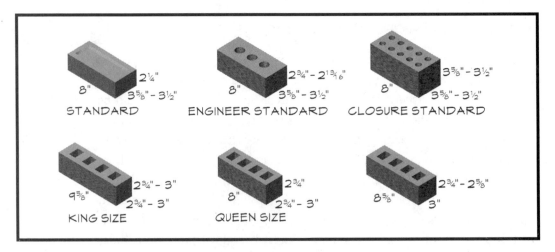

Nonmodular brick sizes with their specified dimensions.

MODULAR BRICK SIZES

Unit Designation	Nominal Dimensions In.			Joint Thickness	Specified Dimensions			Vertical Coursing
	w	h	l		w	h	l	
Modular	4	2⅔	8	⅜	3⅝	2¼	7⅝	3C = 8 in.
				½	3½	2¼	7½	
Engineer Modular	4	3⅕	8	⅜	3⅝	2¾	7⅝	5C = 16 in.
				½	3½	2¹³⁄₁₆	7½	
Closure Modular	4	4	8	⅜	3⅝	3⅝	7⅝	1C = 4 in.
				½	3½	3½	7½	
Roman	4	2	12	⅜	3⅝	1⅝	11⅝	2C = 4 in.
				½	3½	1½	11½	
Norman	4	2⅔	12	⅜	3⅝	2¼	11⅝	3C = 8 in.
				½	3½	2¼	11½	
Engineer Norman	4	3⅕	12	⅜	3⅝	2¾	11⅝	5C = 16 in.
				½	3½	2¹³⁄₁₆	11½	
Utility	4	4	12	⅜	3⅝	3⅝	11⅝	1C = 4 in.
				½	3½	3½	11½	

NON-MODULAR BRICK SIZES

Unit Designation				Joint Thickness	Specified Dimensions			Vertical Coursing
Standard				⅜	3⅝	2¼	8	3C = 8 in.
				½	3½	2¼	8	
Engineer Standard				⅜	3⅝	2¾	8	5C = 16 in.
				½	3½	2¹³⁄₁₆	8	
Closure Standard				⅜	3⅝	3⅝	8	1C = 4 in.
				½	3½	3½	8	
King				⅜	3	2¾	9⅝	5C = 16 in.
					3	2⅝	9⅝	
Queen				⅜	3	2¾	8	5C = 16 in.

Table 3.1 Standard Nomenclature of Brick Sizes. Brick Industry Association.

PAVING BRICK

Flexible, unmortared paving systems are currently favored by the Brick Industry Association and by most manufacturers of paving brick. Given the absence of mortar joints, paving brick is manufactured in ratios of 1:1, 2:1, or 3:1. The most common paver dimension is 4 in. × 8 in. brick (actual size), with a thickness between 1½ in. and 2¼ in. These even ratios facilitate a variety of paving patterns without cutting, and the 4 in. module aligns neatly with any abutting face brick. Common brick paver sizes are indicated in Table 3.2. These pavers are known as "true" pavers, whereas pavers that are sized to accommodate a ⅜ in. mortar joint in a rigid system are called "modular" pavers. Pavers with a thickness of 1¼ in. are called "split" pavers. Many manufacturers offer pavers with beveled top (exposed) edges for visual interest and to minimize the potential for chipped corners.

Specified Face Dimensions (w × l) in.	Specified Thickness (t) in.	Best for Flexible or Rigid Paving System
4 × 4	2¼	Flexible
4 × 8	1½, 2¼, 2⅝, 3	Flexible
3½ × 7½	1½	Rigid
3¾ × 7½	2¼	Rigid
3⅝ × 7⅝	1⅝, 2¼	Rigid
3⅝ × 8	2¼	Rigid
6 × 6	2¼	Flexible
7⅝ × 7⅝	2, 2¼	Rigid
8 × 8	2¼	Flexible
6 × 12	1½	Flexible

Table 3.2 Brick Paver Dimensions.

THE BUSY DESIGNER'S QUICK REFERENCE GUIDE:
Brick Sizes

- The dimensioning of modular brick accounts for the width of the mortar joints and adheres to multiples of 4 in.
- Modular brick is sized to coincide with concrete block coursing.
- Brick dimensions are specified by giving the width, followed by the height and then the length (w × h × l).
- Modular brick is referred to by its nominal size, which varies from its actual and its specified dimensions.
- Nominal size refers to a brick's modularity relative to the 4 in. grid.
- Specified size refers to the dimensions targeted by the manufacturer.
- Actual size refers to the physical dimensions of the brick itself.
- Bricks for use in flexible paving systems are manufactured to specified dimensions that usually adhere to multiples of 4 in., and are called *true pavers*.
- Bricks for use in rigid paving systems are modular and must account for the width of the mortar joint.

BRICK POSITIONS

An individual brick may be positioned so that either its front, top, or end is exposed in a wall. In addition, each of these three faces may be oriented either horizontally or vertically, thus yielding six possible positions for a given brick. Those brick positions oriented in a horizontal alignment are called *stretcher, header, rowlock stretcher,* and *rowlock.* A rowlock stretcher is sometimes called a *shiner.* The two corresponding vertical orientations are the *soldier* and *sailor* positions. Walls composed of stretchers and headers are the most common configuration used in landscape applications. The common bond, the English bond, and the Flemish bond are composed almost entirely of stretchers and headers, with the headers providing a bond between wythes. A cavity wall of rowlock stretchers and rowlocks for bonding will reduce the quantity of brick being used for a wall of the same thickness. Rowlock, soldier, and sailor courses are commonly used to develop interesting capping details where a stone coping is not desired. Both soldier and sailor courses are commonly used to provide stability at the edging of brick walks and patios.

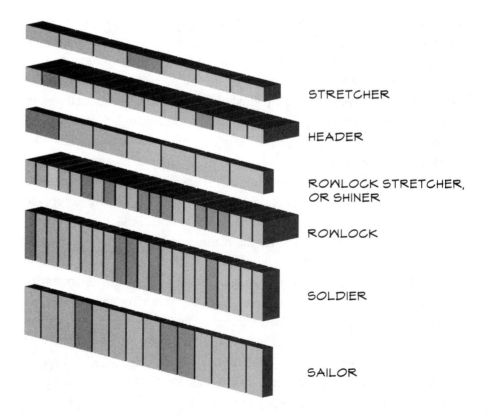

STRETCHER

HEADER

ROWLOCK STRETCHER, OR SHINER

ROWLOCK

SOLDIER

SAILOR

The six possible orientations (positions) of brick within a wall.

> **THE BUSY DESIGNER'S QUICK REFERENCE GUIDE:**
> *Brick Positions*
>
> - A brick's position designation relates to the orientation of its exposed face in a wall.
> - There are six possible brick positions, *stretcher, header, rowlock stretcher, soldier, sailor,* and *rowlock.*
> - A brick in the rowlock stretcher position is sometimes called a *shiner.*
> - Headers are frequently used to provide bonding between wythes.
> - Rowlock stretchers yield a greater surface area in a wall than bricks in the stretcher position. As a result, they are often used to achieve economy of material.
> - Rowlock, soldier, and sailor courses are commonly used to create capping details.

BRICK SHAPES

Shaping brick in molds using the soft-mud process is an ideal method for the production of a variety of brick shapes. The plasticity of clay makes it an ideal material for precisely conforming to any desired shape. The stiff-mud extrusion process, whereby clay is forced through a die to form a continuous column, which in turn is wire-cut into individual green bricks, also lends itself well to the economical production of unique profiles. Brick is extruded in the desired shape by installing a different-shaped die or adapting a standard die. Individual brick manufacturers offer a variety of shapes, depending on which dies they own and use. Although specifying uniquely shaped brick will in all likelihood result in an increase in the cost of labor and tooling associated with setup, the actual increase will depend on the quantity of shaped brick desired. Larger quantities are more economical for the manufacturer to produce than small runs. Furthermore, designers are not limited in choice to currently available shapes. When a project requires a uniquely custom brick profile, designers can work with manufacturers to develop custom shapes but must anticipate even greater costs of production. When contemplating custom shapes, designers must consider the "envelope" established by molds and dies, inasmuch as clay can easily be removed from, but not easily added to, a standard slug shape.

Widely available shapes include half-rounded or fully rounded bullnosed bricks and bricks with a 45-degree chamfered edge. Many brick producers

Uniquely shaped brick adds punctuation to this wall.

offer a range of shaped coping brick and step treads as well. For curved walls, radial bricks are available with both concave and convex (inside and outside curving) surfaces. The nonvisible surface is simply a flat face. These are available in a range of radii. Designers should not overlook the need to specify hybrid transitional bricks whose faces are equal parts radius and tangent. These are required at the point where a curved wall surface meets a flat wall face. Several typical brick shapes for water tables, sills, coping, and treads are shown on the following page. In some cases, the custom profile can be placed on either the stretcher or the header face. With so many options available, it is important for the designer to consult with a manufacturer's representative prior to determining the best shape for a particular situation.

THE BUSY DESIGNER'S QUICK REFERENCE GUIDE:
Brick Shapes

- Bricks shapes are derived either by molding or extrusion.
- Shapes are not widely standardized, and their availability varies from manufacturer to manufacturer.
- Many manufacturers can supply custom shapes according to a designer's specific request.
- Radial bricks are available for either inside or outside curves.
- A variety of radiused and chamfered edges and nosings are widely available.
- Consultation with the manufacturer is strongly recommended when considering the use of shaped brick.

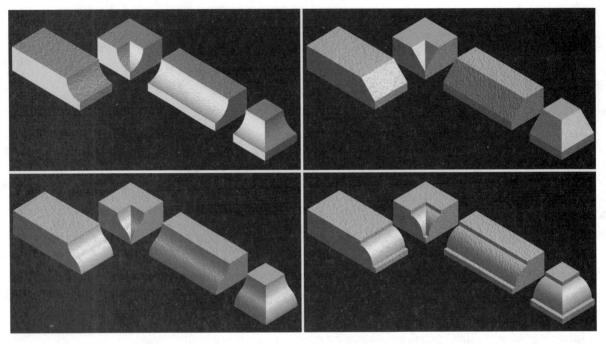

Various available water table brick shapes.

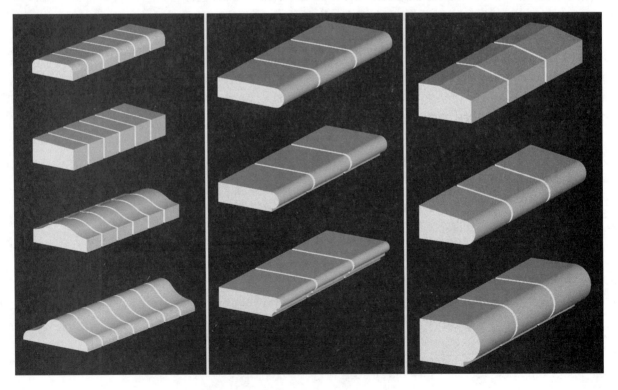

Special shapes for copings, treads and nosings, and sills.

MORTAR

In brick construction, the primary role of mortar joints is adhesion—that is, binding the brick units into a solid, sound masonry structure. Constituting approximately 17% of the surface of a typical brick wall, mortar is a critical yet often overlooked aspect to skillful masonry detailing and design.

Mortar is a mix of portland cement, lime, and sand, or masonry cement and sand, activated and made workable through the introduction of water. Proportions of these components are established by ASTM C270, shown in Table 3.3.

Given the high surface contact of mortar with dry, absorbent bricks during installation, a higher water loss is anticipated with mortar than with concrete. Its water-to-cement ratio must be adjusted accordingly. Highly absorbent brick units (brick capable of absorbing more than 30 g of water per sq. in. per minute) can compromise the curing and ultimate bond strength of mortar. In this case, designers must specify a mortar with a high degree of water retention to counteract the absorbent tendencies of the brick.

PROPORTIONS BY VOLUME (CEMENTITIOUS MATERIALS)

Mortar	Type	Portland Cement or Blended Cement	Masonry Cement and Mortar Cement			Hydrated Lime or Lime Putty	Aggregate Ratio (Measured in Damp, Loose Conditions)
			M	S	N		
Cement Lime	M	1	-	-	-	1/4	
	S	1	-	-	-	over 1/4 to 1/2	
	N	1	-	-	-	over 1/2 to 1 1/4	
	O	1	-	-	-	over 1 1/4 to 2 1/2	
Masonry Cement and Mortar Cement	M	1	-	-	1	-	Not less than 2 1/4 and not more than 3 times the sum of the separate volumes of cementitious materials
	M	-	1	-	-	-	
	S	1/2	-	-	1	-	
	S	-	-	1	-	-	
	N	-	-	-	1	-	
	O	-	-	-	1	-	

Table 3.3 Proportion Specification Requirements. (Copyright ASTM. Reprinted with permission.)

The mortar mixer is a familiar sight during masonry installation.

For consideration by designers, three critical traits of good mortar are its strength, its capacity to bond to the brick units, and its durability. There are four primary classifications of mortar, each intended for a specific set of site conditions and applications. For exterior landscape applications, only three of these four should be considered. *Type N* mortar is an all-purpose medium-strength exterior mortar with excellent resistance to weathering. It should be used for above-grade applications only. *Type S* mortar features greater joint flexibility and high bonding strength. It is recommended for situations where high wind conditions or movement is anticipated or where structural systems require its specification. *Type M* mortar is stronger and more durable and should be the only mortar considered for masonry work that comes in contact with, or extends below, grade. *Type O* mortar is a lower-strength mortar recommended for interior use only.

When preparing the specifications for mortar, the critical standard with which designers should become familiar is ASTM C270, Standard Specification for Mortar for Unit Masonry. Another standard that designers should become acquainted with is ASTM C144, Standard Specification for Aggregate for Masonry Mortar, which deals with the aggregate used in mortar.

Mortar is available in a variety of colors, typically falling within the broad category of earth tones, ranging from light tans to golden ochres to deep reddish browns. Color in mortar is typically achieved via the introduction of admixtures of coloring pigments. These include pure mineral oxides, carbon black, or synthetic colors added to the basic mix.

As in all other considerations, designers must review applicable building codes prior to mortar selection and specification.

THE BUSY DESIGNER'S QUICK REFERENCE GUIDE:
Mortar

- Mortar serves to adhere bricks together and to provide structural support between courses, and impacts the visual characteristics of masonry construction.

- Mortar is a mix of portland cement, lime, and sand, or masonry cement and sand, and water.

- There are three types of mortar used in landscape applications: *Type N* mortar is an all-purpose medium-strength exterior mortar; *Type S* mortar features greater joint flexibility and high bonding strength; and *Type M* mortar is stronger and more durable and should be used for masonry work that comes in contact with grade. *Type O* mortar is a lower-strength mortar not recommended for landscape uses.

- Mortar is available in a variety of colors.

4

This dignified and memorable wall has survived more than a century of exposure to the elements.

Civic gestures in brick serve to uplift and enhance a community's public spaces.

4
APPLICATIONS

BRICK WALLS

Life can be stressful for an exterior brick wall. Incessantly exposed to the elements, it must resist a wide variety of destructive forces throughout its life span. The fact that brick ages so gracefully is a testament to its ability to harmonize with the forces of nature. For designers, brick represents an ideal material for a variety of exterior wall situations. Brick walls make sturdy, long-lasting enclosures and low-maintenance privacy fences. They can serve as seat walls and function well in earth-retaining situations. A time-honored tradition of richly detailed garden walls serves as a physical source of inspiration for landscape designers.

Most students of landscape architecture and design are well acquainted with Thomas Jefferson's serpentine brick wall at the University of Virginia. This masterpiece of early-nineteenth-century single-wythe construction survives today, underscoring the strength, durability, and plasticity of brick as a landscape material. But beyond Jefferson's well-documented creation lies an enormous trove of ingeniously designed and superbly crafted brick walls. No English landscape designed by Sir Edwin Lutyens would be complete without a garden wall of brick, stone, or combinations of the two. The variables of shape, proportion, color, bond, and coping detail provide an endless range of possibilities.

Although simple in nature, brick is capable of achieving richness and detail while performing its structural role.

Exterior brick walls offer the opportunity to link architecture to its site. Frank Lloyd Wright was fond of extending long, low horizontal brick "wing walls" from his buildings far into the site. They are thought to symbolize the building's "arms," embracing the surrounding landscape, uniting building and nature. Matching the design to the building's architectural brick walls in detail, these walls helped to weave architecture and landscape into a coherent whole.

Yet any exterior brick wall, pavement, or installation is only as good as its foundation. This means a foundation that is not only substantial enough to support the load adequately, but one that extends below frost penetration depths and deals effectively with groundwater accumulations. And when a wall is placed in an earth-retention situation, a good foundation must also resist the overturning forces of earth and any surcharge created by retention.

In designing an exterior brick wall, great consideration must be given to mitigating the various forces that water exerts on brick and mortar. While serving as a critical visual component in the overall design of a wall, a coping should also provide effective drainage of storm water away from the wall's surface and interior. The buildup of hydrostatic pressure behind retaining walls and water collection around their footings must be prevented. Even the specific profile of the mortar joints represents an important design decision that will affect a wall's resistance to water penetration.

TYPES OF EXTERIOR WALLS

For landscape applications, there are a few basic options for the design of an exterior brick wall. The following are the most commonly used wall systems in landscape design:

Solid masonry walls

Drainage walls

Pier-and-panel masonry walls

Solid Masonry Walls

The simplest type of exterior wall is the double-wythe solid brick wall. This is a good choice when a wall will have two fair (visible) faces. Composed entirely of brick, the wythes are bonded with headers that span both faces. If only a running bond of stretchers is desired, then the bonding must be achieved through the use of mechanical ties. When only a single fair face of brick is required, such as in a retaining situations, a composite wall should be considered. Composite

The double-wythe brick garden wall represents a solid yet simple detail.

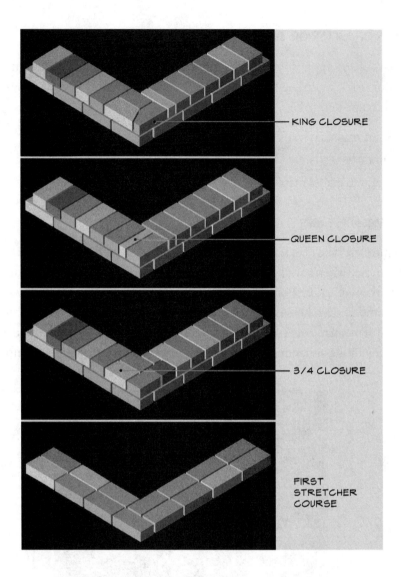

KING CLOSURE

QUEEN CLOSURE

3/4 CLOSURE

FIRST
STRETCHER
COURSE

Three alternatives for turning a 90-degree corner in solid brick construction.

solid masonry walls may be composed of brick bonded to a wythe of concrete block or, less frequently, hollow clay tile, using either brick headers or mechanical ties. The use of mechanical ties limits the designer to either stacked or running bonds, unless cut bricks are used. The use of headers opens up a broader range of options for bonding and decorative diaper patterns (see "Special Techniques," p. 93). Another option for using a solid composite masonry wall arises when the designer requires a wall thickness that is too great for even mechanical ties to span. Brick is tied to both faces of the backup material, which is typically concrete block, structural clay tile, or even cast-in-place concrete. For the last option, continuous vertical metal channels are inserted into the concrete form prior to pouring, permitting a great deal of flexibility in the final placement of the mechanical tie.

Drainage Walls

So named because they feature an air space between the wythes, drainage walls provide a greater economy of material than solid walls. The three basic types of drainage walls are cavity walls, veneer walls, and hollow bonded walls. Each achieves its economy in a different way. The provision of flashing and weep holes in a drainage wall is a critical feature, ensuring that any water intrusion can find a path of exit.

Cavity Walls

The designer should consider a cavity wall when a thickness greater than two wythes is desired. In this type of wall, bricks are typically arranged in a running bond stretcher pattern, as headers are not required. For a situation that calls for two fair faces, the space between the two brick wythes is spanned with a mechanical tie. When only a single fair face is called for, the unseen wythe may be composed of modular concrete block, with the wythes once again bonded with mechanical ties.

Veneer Walls

In veneer walls, as the name suggests, brick is applied as a veneer over a stud backing. This type of wall is not commonly used in landscape applications, but designers should be familiar with the terminology.

Hollow Bonded Walls

Hollow bonded walls feature an internal cavity, with the wythes bonded by a spanning header brick. Hollow bonded walls are commonly constructed with utility size brick (4 × 4 × 12 in., nominal), where the greater brick length permits a greater span and, thus, a thicker wall section. Another typical hollow bonded wall is the all-rowlock wall. Although equal in width to a two-wythe solid wall, the units are turned on edge into a shiner-and-rowlock configuration, in lieu of the more traditional stretcher-and-header combination. The narrower dimension of bricks arranged in a shiner alignment results in a hollow space between the wythes, with the rowlock header spanning the space and providing the bond. The economy results from the smaller quantities of brick required to achieve overall proportions identical to those of a solid wall.

Other Types of Brick Walls

Pier-and-Panel Walls

The pier-and-panel system permits the construction of single-wythe panels by placing reinforced masonry piers at regular intervals. The size and amount of steel reinforcement placed in the piers is contingent on the spacing of the piers (between 8 ft and 16 ft on center), the height of the wall, and the anticipated wind load.

Perforated Brick Walls

Also called pierced walls or brick screen walls, perforated brick walls can provide effective screening with less material where absolute privacy is not required. Among the other advantages of these walls is their ability to permit cooling breezes to pass through. Despite the wall's perforations, the overall wind load is, for all practical purposes, the same as for a solid wall of the

Perforations can add significant visual interest while introducing light and air into walled landscapes.

A common perforated wall detail adapted to a pier-and-panel configuration.

same dimensions. The reduced wind load that results from the perforations is considered to be an even trade-off for the wall's lower total weight. Typically, a perforated wall uses a single-wythe pier-and-panel construction. The perforations result from traditional bond patterns that simply omit the headers. A single wythe is often preferred, because in a traditional double-wythe garden wall, the headers perform the task of bonding its two faces. Lacking its bonding headers, a double-wythe wall must incorporate mechanical ties to bind the faces.

A variety of cross-shaped voids can be achieved by removing combinations of headers *and stretchers* from standard bonding patterns. In these patterns, some of the headers are retained, indicating the advantage of a double-wythe wall where the cutting of half bricks is not required. Still, these cross-shaped perforations should not be dismissed for single-wythe walls, inasmuch as the cutting of half-bricks results in little or no waste.

Perforated panels may also be set into solid walls, as on the following page. In this utilization, the periodic perforations function much like windows in a building, permitting glimpses, light, and air through the wall while sacrificing only a small degree of privacy.

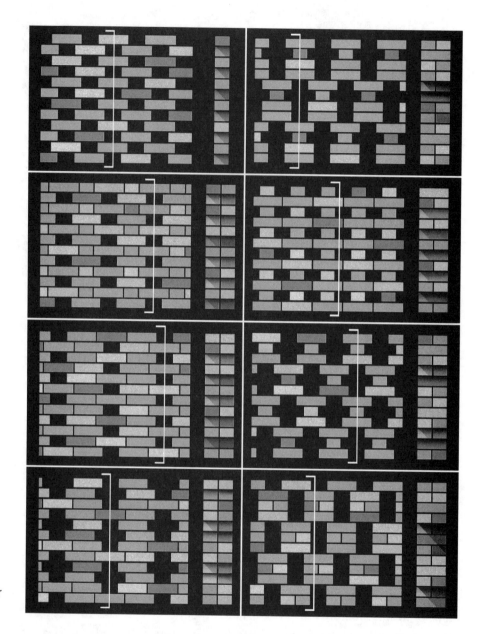

A variety of configurations for perforated brick walls.

Curved Walls

Designers have three options in the design of curving walls. Because of their relatively small unit size, graceful curves can be achieved using standard rectangular bricks. These are economical and work well for larger curves, but their dimensions limit the minimum radius that can be achieved. When tighter curves are desired, brick can be cut to better accommodate the desired radius or the designer can use a specially manufactured radial brick.

The exedra, or semi-circular masonry bench, is curved to encourage discussion, and dates from ancient Greece.

Despite its rectangular shape, brick easily yields graceful curves.

Of these options, the most economical choice is uncut standard brick. However, a radius of less than 5 ft becomes problematic with either a standard 8 in. or 7⅝ in. modular brick. With a running bond pattern, the outer corners of each brick will project beyond the brick beneath it, creating shadowing and an increasingly textured or segmented appearance. Moreover, the angle between any two adjacent bricks results in an excessively wide outside head joint when a radius of less than 5 ft is required. In addition to presenting

Table 4.1 Minimum Radius for a Curved Wall Using Uncut Brick

Unit or Position	Length (in.)	Thickness (in.)	Mortar Joint (in.)	Minimum Radius
Modular	7⅝	3⅝	⅜	6' 6"
			½	4' 11"
Standard	8	3⅝	⅜	6' 9"
			½	5' 2"
Utility	11⅝	3⅝	⅜	9' 8"
			½	7' 3"
Header	⅝	3⅝	⅜	3' 6"
			½	2' 6"
Rowlock or Soldier	2 ¼	3⅝	⅜	2' 2"
			½	1' 8"

Source: Paul H. Perlman, "Choosing Brick for Curved Walls," *Masonry Construction* (Mar. 1992): pp. 103–105.

a generally unattractive appearance, these oversized head joints may prove to be structurally weak. Tight wall radii also tend to emphasize the segmented, nonradial face of standard brick more than larger radii. Simple trigonometry will dictate the minimum radius of a brick wall that will result in head joints of acceptable widths (see Table 4.1).

Walls with tighter radii can be constructed by cutting the back corners of each brick to permit narrower (and more structurally sound) head joints. The visible face of the brick remains untouched, but by removing 1½ in. from the back face, a radius as tight as 2 ft can be achieved with a modular-size brick. Naturally, there will be a measurable increase in cost because of the required cutting, which is labor-intensive. Furthermore, cutting brick does not eliminate the segmented appearance and shadowing of the radius. When a smoother face is desired and the budget permits, the designer should consider specifying radial brick.

The minimum radius that can be achieved by using radial brick is limited only by the dimensions of the individual brick being used. For a wall using modular brick, therefore, a radius as small as 3⅝ in. could, theoretically, be specified. Designers have the option of placing the radius on either or both faces of the curve. Although it achieves a smooth, graceful curve with standard head joint widths, radial brick represents the costliest option. Designers should consider radial bricks as custom-made units and must factor in the added time and cost associated with their production and installation.

A tight radius achieved with nonradial half-bricks with angled lateral faces.

A radial wall composed of stack bond headers accommodates a mature tree in this Kansas City streetscape.

The radial face can be placed on either the outside or inside face of the brick. Note the half-radiused transitional bricks shown in white.

CAPPING AND COPING

The point on a brick wall that is most vulnerable to storm water penetration and subsequent damage is its top. The design of any exterior wall must entail special consideration of the design of the wall's cap or coping. Technically speaking, a cap maintains the same width as the wall, whereas a coping overhangs the wall, much as the eaves of a roof overhang a building, to further distribute rainwater away from the wall. It is typical on a job site to hear masons refer to both methods as "coping."

Caps and copings are not only critical to the visual composition of a brick wall, but they serve to shed water as well.

Although exterior brick walls are routinely coped with brick courses, the designer must keep in mind that a purely horizontal placement of brick and mortar is the configuration most susceptible to water penetration and deterioration. Properly detailed brick copings can be effective in reducing this threat, but a coping of stone or precast concrete probably provides a more reliable detail in preserving and extending the life of a wall. An important detail in the design of any wall cap or coping is the drip-edge cut into the coping's underside. This recess in the cap interrupts the horizontal flow of water, preventing it from seeping into the nearby joint.

When a coping of brick is desired for either design or cost considerations, certain precautions should be taken. In using standard brick, either a header course or a rowlock course is preferred inasmuch as they provide fewer lateral joints for water to cross than does a stretcher course. This, in turn, provides fewer opportunities for water to penetrate into the wall. The orientation of the joints in a header course facilitates drainage where they function much like flues or gutters, whereas the orientation of the lateral joints in a stretcher course serves to impede drainage and retain water. In using standard flat brick for a coping, an adequate cross slope must be pro-

Stone or precast copings feature fewer joints than brick, significantly reducing the potential for water penetration.

vided to shed water. A slope of at least 11% to 13% is generally recommended (just under an inch of slope across an 8 in. thick wall), but the steeper the better. A preferable solution for coping a wall made entirely of brick is to use a specialized coping brick designed for the express purpose of shedding water. Such units include half-round, ogee, saddleback (ridge), bullnose, turtleback (Napoleon) and double-canted bricks. When design considerations and budget permit, a glazed finish on coping bricks will further enhance their resistance to water.

RETAINING WALLS

Few landscape situations challenge designers more than when masonry walls are called upon to retain earth. Natural dynamics work relentlessly to overturn a wall. As groundwater moves horizontally through the soil, it is impounded by a solid masonry wall. There, hydrostatic pressure builds, pushing water directly against the wall, attacking its joints. Freeze-and-thaw cycles in northern climates serve only to increase the pressure on the wall. Without the designer's accounting for these forces, a brick wall in an earth-retaining situation is doomed to eventual failure. The goal of good retaining wall design is not to confront the water head-on, as in building a swimming pool, but rather to drain the wall from behind, dissipating the force of the water. Five measures are required for dealing with this challenging condition.

Waterproofing

To prevent its contact with water, the face of the wall in contact with the soil should be treated with a waterproof compound or covered with a waterproof membrane. Even a dense brick with low permeability will eventually absorb water, given enough time and exposure. Because the buried masonry face is not visible, aesthetics are not a consideration. The more durable the treatment the better. Options for waterproofing a masonry wall include bituminous coatings, asphalt membranes, and elastomeric membranes.

Gravel Backfill

The use of a gravel backfill consists of installing a vertical layer of stone or gravel to keep wet soil away from masonry work. It also facilitates vertical drainage *before the water encounters the masonry units and joints.* A filter that permits water movement, but prevents soil from infilling the gravel's voids, should be placed between the soil and the gravel. If this is omitted, soil will eventually fill the voids, rendering this measure useless. Gravel is resistant to swelling and shrinking during freeze-and-thaw cycles, providing further protection to the wall.

Footing Drains

A drainage system, usually of tile or perforated plastic, is placed at the wall's footing. Used in conjunction with a gravel backfill, it effectively carries away the water that drains vertically through the gravel. It is advisable to place a water-permeable filter atop this drain as well, to prevent sedimentation and clogging.

Weep Holes and Drains

Weep holes are openings, or voids, in a brick wall, whose purpose is the venting and dispersion of any water that finds its way into the wall. Drains serve to reduce or eliminate hydrostatic pressure that may otherwise build up in soil retention situations. To be effective, weep holes must be adequately sloped in section and must "daylight" (penetrate the non-retaining wall face) above finished grade. They can be as simple and reliable as an open (non-mortared) head joint between bricks. Often a small plastic pipe is inserted between the joints, but such pipes are prone to clogging, especially in smaller diameters. Plastic or aluminum weep vents help to camouflage the absence of mortar in a joint and are more reliable. Wicks are sometimes specified to draw moisture out of cavity walls to the walls' exterior. Wicks are typically made of ¼ in. or ⅜ in. diameter rope and are between 10 in. and 12 in. long. Cotton wicks work best; less absorbent nylon wicks are not recommended. Cotton sash cord is frequently used for wicking. If a wick eventually rots, the opening formed in the mortar continues to drain moisture from the cavity. If a wick looses its capacity to transmit water, however, it functions as a plug rather than a drain, defeating the intent of the weep hole altogether. There is some debate that highly absorbent wicks may absorb cement or salts from the wet mortar, greatly impairing their capacity to wick moisture.

For retaining walls with through-wall drains, a screen or mesh covering placed over the retaining-side openings is recommended to prevent their eventual sedimentation and clogging. Drains are usually made from 3 in. diameter pipe and placed between 2 ft and 6 ft apart. Weep holes are typically placed at intervals from 16 in. to 24 in. on center. Local building codes may require a closer spacing, however, and should be consulted during the design phase.

Alternative Backup Material

To prevent brick masonry from coming in contact with retained moisture, consider using brick bonded or veneered to a more economical and more water-resistant backup material. Cast-in-place reinforced concrete or concrete masonry units used in conjunction with the four steps discussed earlier are more cost-effective and may even perform better in terms of overall retaining strength and water repellence. When a brick face is topped with a brick or stone coping, the desired appearance is maintained while water is kept out of contact with the masonry work entirely. Brick is generally more expensive than either cast-in-place concrete or concrete masonry units. It stands to reason that needlessly burying brick represents an unnecessary project cost.

THE BUSY DESIGNER'S QUICK REFERENCE GUIDE:
Brick Walls

- In landscape design the three most common types of walls are solid masonry walls, drainage walls, and pier-and-panel masonry walls.

- Solid masonry walls are composed entirely of brick and mortar.

- Composite solid masonry walls bond brick to a backup material such as cast-in-place concrete or concrete masonry units.

- A drainage wall features an air space within the wall. Three types of drainage walls are cavity walls, veneer walls, and hollow bonded walls.

- Drainage walls must provide for the drainage of water from their interior using a combination of flashing and weep holes.

- Pier-and-panel walls are composed of thin masonry panels supported structurally by reinforced piers.

- A perforated brick wall features a pattern of voids, or openings, in the wall's face.

- Curved walls can be created with either standard rectangular bricks or radial bricks.

- The minimum practical radius available in designing curves composed of standard brick is approximately 5 ft. Tighter radii can be achieved by cutting one or both of the bricks' back corners.

- The smoothest and tightest radii are created with radial brick.

- The radial surface may be either concave, for inside curves, or convex for outside curves.

- Caps and copings both serve a visual function and provide weather resistance.

- Copings are typically composed of brick, stone, or concrete.

- Brick copings using standard shapes should be sloped to encourage drainage.

- A variety of special shapes are available for brick copings.

- Retaining walls place extra lateral force or load on a wall and create greater potential for contact with moisture in soil.

- Retaining walls should be treated with a combination of drainage courses, footing drains, weep holes, through-wall drains, and waterproofing membranes or applications.

- Designers should consider the use of an alternative backup material with greater water resistance than brick masonry when the visual quality is not an issue.

BRICK PAVEMENTS

Brick is a rich and durable choice for a paving material. The look and feel of brick underfoot, (or under *wheel*) provide a friendly visual and tactile experience, giving an effect ranging from casual to elegant. Brick paths, walks, and terraces enrich designed landscapes and gardens with a quality that few other pavements can approach. But brick paving is not limited to the garden path. Brick streets were once a familiar sight in almost every American downtown. Many are still intact despite decades of increasingly heavy use and exposure to the weather and pollution. Less apparent is the fact that many downtown streets still retain brick pavements *beneath* more recent layers of asphalt resurfacing. Those few remaining brick streets are now celebrated as unique and cherished reminders of a time that featured a less synthetic and more skill-

Brick pavements offer a wealth of design opportunities in the landscape.

Every element in this landscape, from the plant materials to the brick pavement and even the level of maintenance, suggests sincere and thoughtful care of this garden. (Courtesy of Glen-Gery Corporation. Photograph by Tim Schoon, York, Pennsylvania.)

fully crafted environment. "Charming bungalow on a brick street." Today's sharp realtors are quick to grasp the real and perceived value of brick pavement over more commonly used materials.

Although brick is currently used on a somewhat limited basis for paving where vehicular circulation is anticipated, its special qualities remain unchallenged. Monument Circle in Indianapolis, the physical and symbolic center of the state of Indiana, is paved almost entirely with brick, underscoring the site's geographic and political prominence. Brick is often used to announce pedestrian crosswalks in an otherwise ordinary roadway pavement. More than simply a visual gesture, the change in texture and the resulting tire-sound serve to warn drivers that they are entering a potential pedestrian conflict zone, encouraging them to slow down. Office buildings and corporate headquarters routinely rely on brick-paved plazas to enhance their primary entrance/auto court areas. Brick serves as the "doormat" of the corporate villa, welcoming visitors and VIPs. When brick is used in the pavement, the message is clear. The rich color and texture of brick underfoot often indicates that you have left a commonplace area and entered into a landscape of a heightened significance.

Brick used to create the "welcome mat" for a large corporate facility. (Courtesy of Endicott Clay Products Company.)

A rigid pavement intended to stand up to the stresses of the urban environment.

The unfortunate fate of many rigid pavements in cold climates.

PAVING SYSTEMS

There are two broad categories of brick pavements, rigid and flexible. In a rigid paving system, the joints between the individual pavers are filled with mortar and the bricks are typically set into a mortar setting bed. The entire pavement area rests atop a base of rigid concrete and functions as a single unit, much like a piece of peanut brittle. The purpose of rigid pavements is to prevent water penetration through their water-resistant mortar joints. This system works well as long as *each and every joint* remains sound and water-tight. Unfortunately, expansive areas of rigid pavement are relatively weak in their overall tensile strength and are unlikely to survive prolonged exposure to weathering and traffic wholly intact. With rigid pavements, some degree of joint failure is not only a distinct possibility, but perhaps a predictable eventuality. Once a mortar joint is compromised and water is permitted to penetrate, damage is likely in the form of efflorescence, spalling, cracking, or dislodged pavers. The long-term presence of water in the joint, combined with the added destructive force of freeze-and-thaw cycles, will invariably result in some degree of damage to the pavement.

In landscape applications, rigid systems work best in conditions that are sheltered from the weather, such as by porches, or in southern climates that are not subjected to frequent and repeated freeze-and-thaw cycles. In designing a rigid pavement system intended for harsher climates, providing adequate slopes for rapid and efficient drainage will prolong the life of the system. In broad paved areas, such as plazas, it is recommended that the pavement's longitudinal joints be oriented in the same direction as the drainage so as to minimize potential for impeding the runoff. For linear walks, the long joints should run perpendicular to the direction of travel, facilitating the lateral drainage of the pavement. In northern climates where snow and ice are common, significant problems with rigid brick pavements arise where salt is used as a melting agent. Salt compounds are extremely destructive to masonry installations, especially when they are dissolved in rain or melting snow and permitted prolonged contact with the mortar joints.

A surface of rigid brick pavers has different inherent expansion and moisture capacities than the rigid concrete base on which it is installed. These differences are magnified in large areas of continuous pavement. The zone of contact between these two layers must permit differential movement, or the concrete will transfer the stress to the brick and the mortar joints. To mitigate this stress, the designer must provide expansion joints a maximum of 16 ft apart. For larger spans where expansion joints are not possible, a membrane layer, known as a *bond break,* typically 15 lb felt or plastic sheeting, allows the two rigid layers to move independently.

A second broad category is *flexible paving,* in which no mortar is used between the individual pavers. Whereas rigid pavements must be supported by a rigid concrete base, flexible systems can be placed over either rigid or flexible base materials. Typically, sand is swept into the hand-tight joints to minimize the potential for horizontal movement. A flexible paving system acknowledges and accommodates the likelihood of movement by permitting movement between the individual pavers. Water is allowed to penetrate the joints and is drained at both the surface and the base levels. Flexible paving

A flowing pathway using a nonmortared (flexible) pavement system. (Courtesy of Pine Hill Brick Company.)

systems do not eliminate maintenance, but allow substantially easier replacement of damaged or dislodged pavers. When flexible pavements are used, special consideration must be given to containing the units and controlling their movement, because they are essentially "floating" atop a base layer. Lacking mortared joints, the individual pavers are more prone to movement, especially where traffic is expected. A stable, rigid edging or curbing material along the entire perimeter of a brick pavement will serve to prevent horizontal movement or slippage of the hand-tight units. Typical options for curbing areas of brick pavement are stone, precast concrete, cast-in-place concrete, metal edging or soldier courses of the brick itself. The soldier courses may be set in gravel where light traffic is expected but should be embedded in concrete where greater durability is required. A number of commercially made metal edge treatments are widely available. Metal edgings are typically held in place with spikes driven into the base. Because the hand-tight joints permit the seepage of water, drainage must be provided at the uppermost impervious level.

BASES

Brick pavements require base courses for three primary reasons. First, a base provides structural strength and stability to the pavers. Another function of the base, especially in flexible paving systems, is to facilitate drainage, either through its permeability or via mechanical means. Finally, the base course serves to mitigate any surface irregularities that may occur either in the brick itself or as a result of the shrinking or swelling of the earth owing to varying moisture content and freeze-and-thaw cycles.

Bases for Rigid Pavement Systems

When a rigid pavement is called for, it must be set on a rigid base of reinforced concrete. The more brittle rigid pavements are not compatible with flexible bases of sand or gravel which are prone to movement. A rigid concrete base is reinforced exactly as a concrete walk or drive would be, depending on its anticipated traffic load.

Bases for Flexible Pavement Systems

A flexible pavement may be set on a flexible base or, when added strength or stability is required, on a rigid base. The most durable base for a flexible pavement is a rigid base. It is similar in composition to the rigid base described for rigid pavement systems, with the difference being the setting bed. A rolled bituminous setting bed approximately ¾ in. thick often replaces the mortar setting bed used in rigid pavement systems. When flexible, hand-tight pavers are to be set on rigid, impervious base materials such as asphalt or concrete, special consideration must be given to drainage. Because the hand-tight joints of the paving brick will admit water to the bed level, it is critical to drain this water. Drains at the bed level, or double-height drains (drains set at the surface level with vented sides at the bed level) and/or weep holes provided in the edging material are required to prevent the long-term retention of water within the open joints and beneath the pavers.

Another reliable option for a flexible pavement is a semirigid base. This is typically a course of asphalt concrete road pavement or asphalt. A semirigid base should be used only with flexible paving systems, as it lacks the structural support required for brittle, mortared rigid pavements. A rolled hot-mix bituminous setting bed is placed atop the asphalt base. This functions much as a mortar setting bed and is typically between ¾ in. and 1 in. in thickness. It provides the added advantage of flexibility when the bricks are leveled during installation, yielding a smoother, more even surface, a clear advantage when safety or snow removal is a concern.

A flexible base of crushed stone, gravel, stone screenings, compacted sand, or a loose cement-sand mix is a less costly option than a rigid or semirigid base. These porous bases also facilitate drainage better than impervious concrete or asphalt bases, although unwashed gravel and stone screenings provide somewhat less porosity. The trade-off lies in their reduced carrying capacity. An ideal base material is crushed stone, especially a mix that is not graded to a specific size range. When used with a sand bed, it constitutes a reliable and popular detail. The inclusion of a broader range of aggregate sizes, including fine material, permits the sharp-edged aggregate to "lock into" a matrix, providing better long-term stability than graded gravel. Bank-run or river-washed aggregates are also strong, porous base materials, but these lack the capacity of crushed stone to interlock pieces with one another. Their smooth, rounded surfaces resist interlocking. Even a fine pea gravel lacks the ability to be adequately

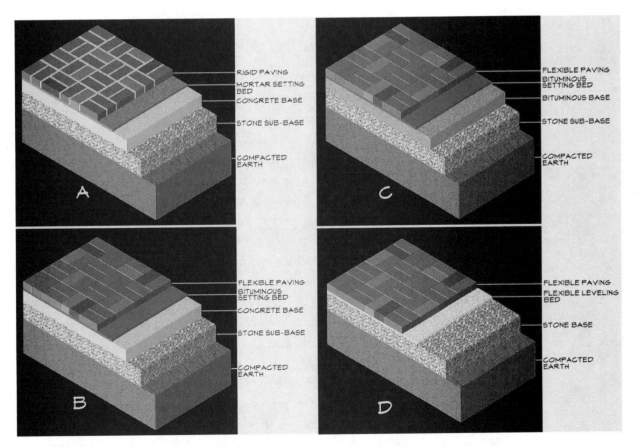

The four basic brick paving systems. (A) Rigid paving over a rigid base. (B) Flexible paving over a rigid base. (C) Flexible paving over a semirigid base. (D) Flexible paving over a flexible base.

compacted and stabilized. Although providing excellent drainage and flexibility, these aggregates do not offer the same stability as crushed stone. Sand bases should be limited to use beneath residential walks and patios only. As a base material, sand retains its inherent instability throughout the life of an installation. It neither compacts over time nor achieves any measurable degree of cementing or interlocking. It can shift as easily after 25 years as on the day it is installed. This condition may be acceptable for a residential installation when the owner is willing to maintain the pavement by periodically reinstalling uneven bricks. A dry mix of cement and sand provides only slightly greater stability than sand alone. A high ratio of sand to cement (one part portland cement to three to six parts sand) permits the base to retain porosity and avoid bonding with the brick pavers, but prevents the material from truly setting up. Staining, in the form of efflorescence, is a likely problem with this choice, making a base of sand alone a superior option.

Design Considerations

When considering a pavement of brick, and again when determining its method of installation, designers must keep a few simple but critical guidelines in mind. First, the earth is not static, but undergoes frequent movement. The geologic and seasonal mechanisms of the earth are constantly in motion. Depending on their content, different soil types expand and contract with water content to greater or lesser degrees (clay more than loam, loam more than sand, for example). Climate is another factor in soil movement. Because water increases in volume when frozen, soils in northern climates shrink and swell with the freeze-thaw cycle, often several times a season. The roots of nearby (or not so nearby) trees can uplift pavements with their slow but relentless growth. Seismic zones, surprisingly widespread throughout North America, can subtly, or sometimes drastically, alter the surface configuration of a site. All of these contingencies suggest a paving material and method of installation that is flexible and can accommodate to a certain amount of movement. Flexible brick pavements, with their open "hand-tight" swept joints rather than a rigid matrix of mortared joints, should be considered where significant movement is anticipated.

Another important fact for the designer to bear in mind is that horizontally laid paving brick experiences a different set of stresses than does vertically stacked brick in walls or columns. Pavements endure the effects of traffic, are exposed to greater weathering, and are generally slower to drain water than vertical installations. Paving bricks must be fired to a harder state and capable of greater water resistance, a factor known as absorption. Anyone who has attempted to create a charming patio from salvaged building brick has quickly learned a hard lesson. Soft brick, intended for walls and buildings, has difficulty surviving the added stresses inherent in a paving condition and invariably degrades rapidly. Water is the enemy of all brick, but especially unsheltered brick arranged in a horizontal alignment. In its normal cycle of freezing and thawing, water can work quickly to degrade both the brick and its mortar joints. Only brick that has an absorption rate of 8% or less should be used as a horizontal paving surface.

Safety and traction are also important considerations. Some finishes become quite slippery when wet. Accidents and lawsuits are likely to result from the use of any paving material, including brick, that becomes excessively "slippery when wet." Fortunately, there are several brick surfaces that offer a high degree of traction. The common wire-cut finish, a feature of many extruded paving bricks, provides excellent traction. A variety of other surface textures are available from different manufacturers. The designer should examine a manufacturer's samples carefully when considering the relative safety of a paving brick in wet conditions.

Surface texture, joint size, and method of installation must also be considered when designing for the disabled. Individuals using crutches, canes, and wheelchairs must be permitted to move easily and safely across all paving surfaces. Likewise, bicycle tires, high-heeled shoes, baby strollers, and snowplow blades should be universally accommodated in any pavement design. Unfortunately, each of these issues is commonly cited as a reason to use alternative pavements in lieu of brick. Yet each of these specific issues can be successfully addressed with the proper detailing and installation of a brick pavement.

Finally, a well-designed brick pavement drains water efficiently. Storm water runoff must be considered integral to the paving system during the design process. Not even the least absorbent brick can tolerate extended submersion beneath water and ice. Surface and subsurface drainage design, along with appropriate pavement detailing, can minimize the risk of water-related pavement failure.

The challenge to the designer is to fit the solution to the situation. The entrance to a heavily traffiked office building calls for a pavement that is absolutely stable, well drained, and evenly graded. Yet a bit of unevenness can provide charm and may even be preferable for a rustic, meandering path through a residential garden. Cost, safety, durability, and aesthetic considerations each play a role in determining which brick paving system best suits a particular project.

STANDARD BRICK PAVERS

Given the stress and abuse that a pavement must endure, it is important to specify a brick that will survive such treatment. A dense, low-absorption brick should be specified. For most applications, a brick that meets ASTM C902 (Standard Specification for Pedestrian and Light Traffic Paving Brick), Class SX, Type I, will suffice. For heavier traffic areas, pavers that meet ASTM C1272 should be used. A typical range of brick pavers is shown on the following page.

PAVING PATTERNS

Most experienced designers are familiar with a number of optional patterns for brick pavements. But designers are by no means restricted to the "standards." Brick paving patterns are limited only by the creativity of the designer and the project budget. When a custom, one-of-a-kind appearance is sought, designers may consider looking beyond the more traditional, oft-repeated patterns.

Too often the choice of a paving pattern is thought of as a purely visual consideration. This decision carries with it greater implications of pavement stability and installation cost, however. The long-term durability and stability of any brick construction result in part from the degree of interlocking achieved with the individual units. In choosing a paving pattern, it is important to consider the length of straight, uninterrupted joints. A stack bond pattern achieves virtually no interlocking whatsoever. Long, straight joint lines project in both directions of the pattern, permitting slippage both lengthwise and laterally. The basketweave pattern is a more popular configuration, but analysis of the joints also reveals long, uninterrupted joints in both directions. Both patterns are fine when used in relatively small areas bordered by a secure edging. When they are applied to long linear areas of pavement, such as roads and walks, the designer may consider rotating the pattern 45 degrees to the direction of flow.

The most common pattern is undoubtedly the running bond. It provides adequate interlocking of the brick units, and the pattern results in

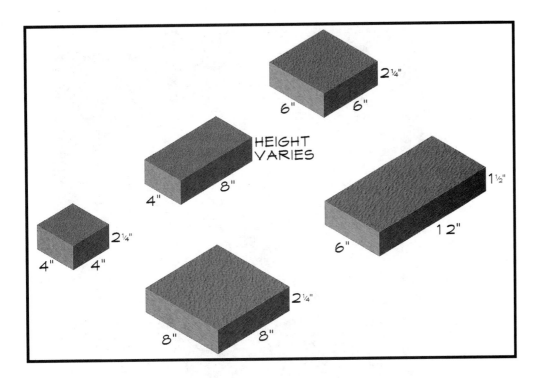

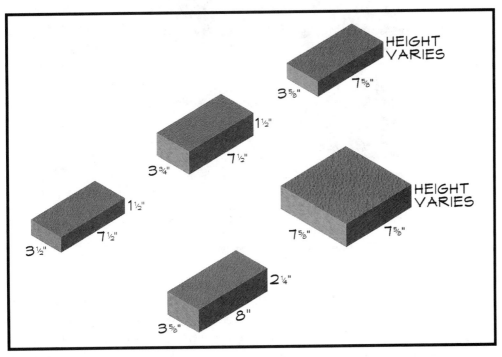

Several common true paver sizes. These pavers are intended for use in flexible pavement systems with no allowance for mortar joints. *(Bottom)* Common modular paver sizes. These pavers are best used in rigid pavement systems. Their dimensions accommodate a mortar joint between pavers.

A variety of running bond pavements.

long joints in only one direction. It is recommended that the long joints be aligned perpendicular to the primary direction of traffic flow. This measure not only minimizes the potential for movement, but many designers prefer it for visual reasons. If there are even slight irregularities in the nonstaggered joints, they will be far more apparent to the eye if they run in the same direction as traffic.

Examples of herringbone pavements.

The herringbone pattern is an extremely stable configuration. Evaluation of the jointing reveals no long joints in any direction. It achieves a high degree of stability through its interlocking and provides a great deal of visual interest. This pattern is often recommended for flexible brick pavements subjected to vehicular traffic. The herringbone may be installed at either 90-degree or 45-degree angles to its edges.

A portfolio of variations on the basketweave pattern.

The basketweave pattern, as well as its many variations, has proven to be among the most popular, especially among do-it-yourselfers. It may be installed with great efficiency, yielding little waste and requiring few or no cuts. It does result in long, straight joints with little interlocking of individual units, but some of its variations mitigate this problem. The basketweave pattern is equally at home in the corporate landscape and in the backyard.

A means of economizing in pavement design is to minimize any required cuts.

In paving large areas, the labor costs associated with the frequent cutting of brick can be a significant determinant in the selection of a pattern. When precision is important, brick cutting is performed by hand, on-site, using a diamond-tipped saw blade. Brick should be wet cut, because significant health issues are linked to the airborne dust generated by dry cutting. Each brick must first be marked, then carefully aligned and cut. Unless the unused portion of the cut brick coincidentally fits another void, it either becomes waste or is stockpiled for future cutting. The process is labor-intensive and slows the installation of a paving project. When carefully planned, a good design will minimize any necessary cutting along its edges. It is particularly critical to avoid situations requiring small sliver cuts to complete a pattern, as they are prone to crack or become dislodged.

When properly dimensioned, the stack bond and the basketweave patterns can be installed in rectangular areas of pavement with no cutting whatsoever. The running bond pattern requires cutting along one of its edges only, ideally resulting in half-bricks yielding little or no waste. When oriented 90 degrees to its perimeter, the herringbone pattern may also require only the cutting of half-bricks. Any pattern rotated 45 degrees to its edging, however, will require a greater number of cuts. Where additional loading is anticipated, brick may be turned on edge, significantly increasing its flexural strength. With some adjustment, many standard paving patterns can be configured with the pavers set on edge.

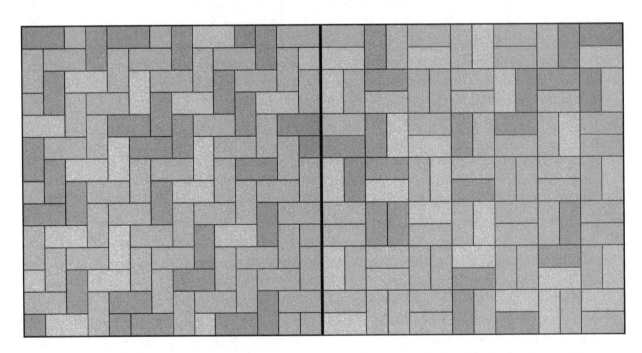

These three pages show a variety of common and not-so-common paving patterns. Note that the final three patterns on page 80 use brick with an exposed stretcher configuration for greater pavement strength.

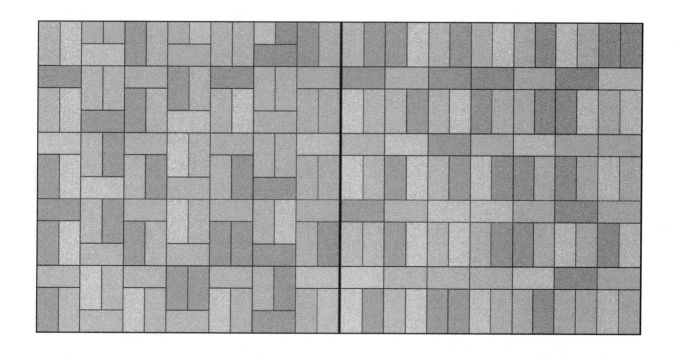

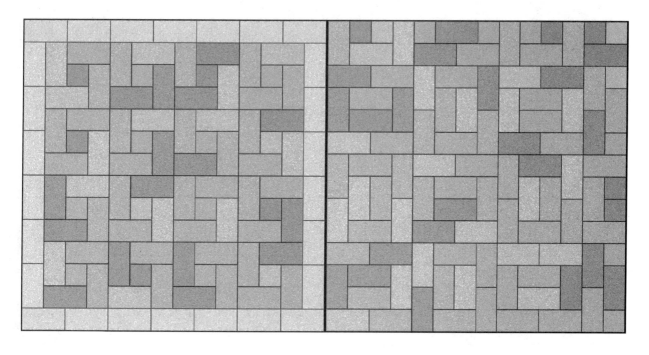

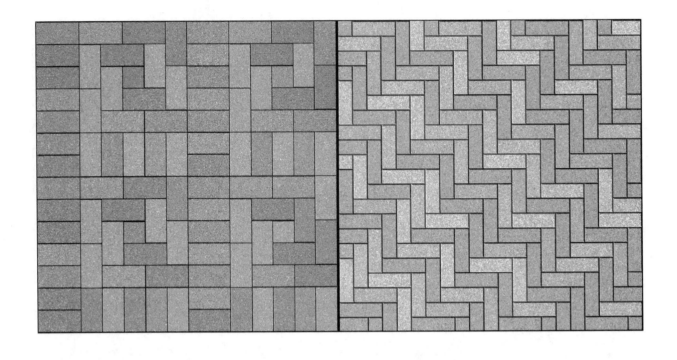

> **THE BUSY DESIGNER'S QUICK REFERENCE GUIDE:**
> *Brick Pavements*
>
> - The two types of brick paving systems are *rigid* pavements and *flexible* pavements.
> - A rigid pavement must be supported by a rigid base of concrete.
> - A flexible pavement may be supported by a base that is rigid, semirigid, or flexible.
> - In rigid pavement systems, the joints between the brick pavers are mortared and the brick are set into a mortar setting bed.
> - Flexible pavements feature hand-tight joints without mortar.
> - Soil movement, owing to freeze-and-thaw cycles, and water penetration are common causes of failure in rigid pavement systems.
> - Traction, especially in wet conditions, is an important safety consideration in the selection of brick pavers.
> - Paving bricks are exposed to water for longer periods than bricks in a vertical wall and must be fired to a harder state.
> - Salvaged building brick is not suitable for use in exterior pavements.
> - Designers must ensure the rapid drainage of any paving system.
> - The choice of paving pattern will affect both the stability and the cost of the installation.
> - Using a herringbone pattern in flexible brick pavements subjected to vehicular traffic will add stability.
> - Designs that require excessive on-site cutting and/or a significant amount of waste material will result in higher installation costs.

BRICK STEPS

Few brick applications require the designer to place as high a priority on safety considerations as does the design of exterior steps. Not only must a set of steps function safely in the landscape for able-bodied individuals, but they must also satisfy the special needs of individuals with temporary or permanent disabilities. Particular attention should be paid to providing a distinct visual contrast where there is a transition from a flat pavement to a vertical grade change, such as in steps. In addition, attention must be given to traction on steps in wet or snowy conditions. Smooth brick finishes that become excessively slippery in the rain are unsuitable for steps.

Exterior steps pose a challenge to the designer. Safety, durability, and beauty must each be given a high priority.

A rigid system incorporating mortared joints, along with a rigid reinforced concrete base, is recommended for the design of brick steps. For safety, stability is a primary requirement for well-detailed steps. A tread or nosing that has become even partially dislodged is a considerable safety hazard in an exterior environment. The extra stresses on steps, particularly when a person is descending, require a detail that is stable and sound. Even in the design of the most casual of residential garden steps, flexible paving bricks can be a hazard. If a flexible pavement is absolutely required, a rigid, secure curb or edging is necessary, especially along the nosing edge. And to prevent the edging from impounding water, weep holes are required.

Even when an otherwise flexible paving system is called for, rigid steps provide the greatest degree of safety and durability. (Courtesy of Pine Hall Brick Company.)

These brick steps are well lit and firmly secured. They offer no protruding nosing to trip on. A contrasting nosing color would further call out each step to those with visual impairments.

Under the right lighting conditions, the treads of any set of steps can easily become visually indistinct. When sharp shadows are absent, steps constructed of a monochromatic material can blend together visually. Where even moderate amounts of pedestrian traffic are anticipated, a nosing brick of a contrasting color and texture on each tread is recommended, which will help to distinguish each ensuing change of grade.

The treads should be sloped no less than ¼ in. per ft to encourage rapid drainage of water. As in brick pavements, the joints should be oriented in the direction of flow to help direct water down the wash of the tread, rather than impede it. To prolong the life of the steps, the tread bricks should extend

This arrangement of tread and riser invites water into these masonry steps should the joint fail. A better configuration would extend the tread under the riser.

under the riser bricks, resulting in a vertical rather than a horizontal joint face. The opposite configuration, in which the riser brick extends behind the tread brick, creates an undesirable horizontal joint face and much greater potential for water penetration should the mortar joint be compromised. A tread composed of a full stretcher, plus a stretcher that is half-lapped under the riser, yields a comfortable tread width of approximately 12 in.

Tread bricks may be placed in either a rowlock or a header configuration. The former is stronger, but the latter uses fewer bricks. The design of brick steps also represents an opportunity to take full advantage of unique nosing designs, such as bullnoses and bevels. These slight overhangs can create distinctive shadows and enhance the visibility of the grade changes.

The standards established by the Americans with Disabilities Act of 1990 (ADA) require that a nosing's overhang not exceed 1½ in. (38 mm), with a radius at its leading edge no greater than ½ in. (13 mm). Further, they state that the underside of the nosing should not be an abrupt protrusion, posing an opportunity for catching one's toe. Instead, the nosing should accomplish the transition back to the riser at an angle of not less than 60 degrees.

A common problem area is the interface between the pavement and a handrail. The forces exerted on a handrail are transferred to its weakest point. Without a substantial footing, even slight movement of the handrail can work

The shadow created by the gently radiused nosing brick calls attention to the change of grade in this landscape. (Courtesy of Endicott Clay Products Company.)

The anatomy of brick steps. Rigid masonry steps combined with a flexible pavement. Note the realtionship between treads and risers. Even should a joint fail, the wash of the steps will drain water away.

like a lever, causing rigid pavements to crack. Without proper sealing, this joint provides an avenue for water infiltration. The problem can be resolved by anchoring the handrail in the adjacent earth or into a concrete curb or cheek wall, or by providing expansion capability at the base of the handrail.

> ## THE BUSY DESIGNER'S QUICK REFERENCE GUIDE:
> ### Brick Steps
>
> - Safety is the overriding issue in the design of exterior steps, brick or otherwise.
> - A rigid step system (mortared joints) is preferred, even when the adjacent pavement is a flexible system.
> - Tread bricks should extend beneath the riser bricks to create a horizontally oriented joint between the two.
> - Treads should be sloped ¼ in. per ft to facilitate drainage.
> - The forces imposed on handrails require that they be adequately supported and that no movement is transmitted to the rigid brick step system.
> - Custom tread bricks are widely available, but the designer should consider the step standards established by the Americans with Disabilities Act (ADA) before specifying a nosing shape.

WATER FEATURES

Throughout this text, water is treated as the archenemy of brick construction. Yet when suitably detailed, brick can be the primary or a contributing component in the design of fountains and pools. Because of its relatively small unit size, brick can create visually captivating effects as water flows and splashes across its textured surfaces. Water highlights the natural colors of brick, imparting even richer and deeper earth tones than when it is dry. Many landscape architects have exploited the richness that brick brings to the design of lively water features. Innovative brick constructions add sorely needed sparkle and life to urban environments across America, and the profession is continuing to discover ways of making masonry and water compatible and complementary landscape components.

The designer should consider the effects of constant exposure to water, much as if it were severe weather. Choice of material, joint design, and craftsmanship each contribute to the ability of masonry to stand up to water. The Brick Industry Association recommends specifying a brick that conforms to ASTM C902, Class SX. Such bricks are rated to resist damage when saturated, even where freezing is likely. Opportunities for water intrusion must be eliminated, with all mortar joints full and free of voids. Any masonry water

When proper precautions are taken during the design phase, water and masonry may be combined.

A fantasy waterscape composed entirely of brick masonry. (Courtesy of Endicott Clay Products Company.)

basin should have the capacity to be drained completely dry during cold seasons. When brick is used horizontally as an element in a water feature, care must be taken to ensure adequate slope (no less that ¼ in. per ft) to a drain. Provided that designers take a few simple precautions, there is no reason to avoid using brick in the design of water features.

THE BUSY DESIGNER'S QUICK REFERENCE GUIDE:
Water Features

- Water is a potentially destructive element to brick and mortar. Masonry used in the design of water features must be carefully detailed to minimize extended exposure to water.
- Water both enlivens and deepens the rich hues of brick.
- Horizontal brick surfaces should be adequately sloped for efficient drainage.
- Masonry water basins should have the capacity to be drained in the winter.

COLUMNS, PIERS, AND PILASTERS

One of brick's inherent strengths is its ability to carry compressive loads. When used as a vertical column of support, brick is truly flexing its muscle. Beyond its physical structural capacities, designers value brick columns for their *visual* strength as well. Brick simply *appears* solid and stable in support roles. Whether used to support fences or luminaires, in pier-and-panel masonry walls or in bollards, or as supports for pergolas and arbors, stacked columns of brick function superbly as elements in a built landscape.

DEFINITIONS

According to the Brick Industry Association, a *pier* is an isolated column of masonry that is not bonded to masonry at its sides and a *pilaster* is a wall portion projecting from either or both wall faces and serving as a vertical column and/or beam. Columns and piers are freestanding elements. Pilasters are integrated into the wall itself. As landscape elements, columns are used in the vertical support of arbors, trellises, pergolas, gazebos, luminaires, signage, or identification or may be essentially decorative, freestanding elements.

A stately column of brick serves as a sentry to this elegant residence.

MASONRY COLUMNS

Lacking lateral components such as a wall, columns do not require the same degree of resistance to overturning as do piers and pilasters. Unless they are tied to an element with a high wind profile, reinforcing is not typically required in landscape columns, as steel adds very little to the supportive strength of a masonry column. The structural role of columns is primarily to withstand compression; that is, they typically support a load placed atop

The bonding for a variety of freestanding columns and piers.

them. In architectural applications these loads can be quite substantial. In landscape applications such loads, typically, are significantly lower than in architecture. The spacing of piers or columns supporting relatively minor loads, such as the beams of arbors or pergolas, depends more on the structural spanning capacity of the beam being supported than on the masonry itself. In these situations wind loads are minor, though not negligible, and the weight of wood or metal trelliswork rarely approaches the compressive threshold of a properly dimensioned brick column. A more important factor is the tie between the trelliswork and the pier. Both wind and potential seismic activity require a mechanical tie to prevent dislodging the cross member from its masonry support. A typical solution is an embedded lag bolt with washer and nut, sized to accommodate the weight and dimension of the trellis.

PIER-AND-PANEL WALLS

In a pier-and-panel wall, the piers are providing lateral support rather than supporting a vertical load. Their job is to prevent the wall from tipping over as a result of wind pressure or other impacts. With the piers providing most of the structural support, the panels may be as thin as a single wythe. A pier-and-panel system can thus be considered an economical alternative to a straight wall with a continuous section of two or more wythes. Table 4.2 shows the recommended spacing of horizontally oriented reinforcing steel for panels at spans of 8 ft, 10 ft, 12 ft, 14 ft, and 16 ft. Table 4.3 provides recommendations for vertical reinforcing, using the same spans at wall heights of 4 ft, 6 ft, and 8 ft. Note that these tables are for nonretaining conditions only.

Table 4.2 Panel Wall Reinforcing Steel. (Used with permission of the Brick Industry Association.)

| Wall Span (ft) | Vertical Spacing (in.) | | | | | | | | |
| | Wind Load (10 psf) | | | Wind Load (15 psf) | | | Wind Load (20 psf) | | |
	A	B	C	A	B	C	A	B	C
8	45	30	19	30	20	12	23	15	9.5
10	29	19	12	19	13	8.0	14	10	6.0
12	20	13	8.5	13	9	5.5	10	7.0	4.0
14	15	10	6.5	10	6.5	4.0	7.5	5.0	3.0
16	11	7.5	5.0	7.5	5.0	3.0	6.0	4.0	2.5

A = 2 No. 2 bars
B = 2 3/16 in. diameter wires
C = 2 9 gauge wires

Table 4.3 Pier Reinforcing Steel. (Used with permission of the Brick Industry Association.)

Wall Span (ft)	Wind Load (10 psf) Wall Height (ft)			Wind Load (15 psf) Wall Height (ft)			Wind Load (20 psf) Wall Height (ft)		
	4	6	8	4	6	8	4	6	8
8	2 # 3	2 # 4	2 # 5	2 # 3	2 # 5	2 # 6	2 # 4	2 # 5	2 # 5
10	2 # 3	2 # 4	2 # 5	2 # 4	2 # 5	2 # 7	2 # 4	2 # 6	2 # 6
12	2 # 3	2 # 5	2 # 6	2 # 4	2 # 6	2 # 6	2 # 4	2 # 6	2 # 7
14	2 # 3	2 # 5	2 # 6	2 # 4	2 # 6	2 # 6	2 # 5	2 # 5	2 # 7
16	2 # 4	2 # 5	2 # 7	2 # 4	2 # 6	2 # 7	2 # 5	2 # 6	2 # 7

Within shaded areas 12 in. × 16 in. pier required. All other values obtained with 12 in. × 12 in. pier (see Fig. 4.41).

Reinforced masonry construction will greatly increase resistance to overturning and thus permit greater heights. Steel reinforcement adds little or nothing to masonry's compressive strength, but increases its bending strength tremendously. Although it is recommended that designers consult a structural engineer for any reinforcing design, there are a couple of basic rules to bear in mind. Vertical steel members should be no less than .25% and no greater than 4% of a column's total area. Codes may require a minimum of four bars in columns and piers. Given the generally lower heights and reduced loads of most (but not all) landscape masonry walls, multiple-wythe solid masonry construction does not always require supporting pilasters. The design of all walls and piers/pilasters should be undertaken using actual loads in conformance with the appropriate regulating codes: American Concrete Institute (ACI) 530, American Society of Civil Engineers (ASCE) 5/TMS 402.

Capping or coping of all vertical masonry constructions, including columns, piers, and pilasters, should not be overlooked. Any horizontal masonry construction that permits water to remain for an extended length of time represents a potential for intrusion and system failure. Not only is masonry prone to water intrusion, but rusted steel reinforcing (resulting from exposure to internal water) will expand in volume, exerting pressure from within the masonry construction, causing cracking and/or joint failure.

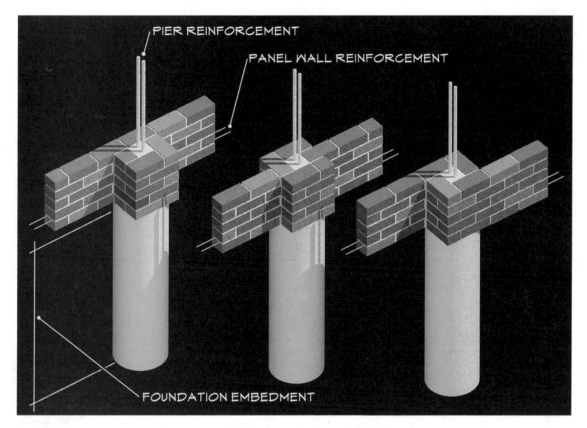

Three options for pier-and-panel garden walls.

FOUNDATIONS

Foundations for vertical piers and pilasters are typically reinforced cast-in-place concrete. Water is the enemy of all masonry systems, and concrete does a superior job of resisting the erosive forces of freezing and water penetration. However, foundations of concrete masonry units or low-porosity SW brick combined with type M or S mortar may also be used, although this may pose a structural problem depending on soil types and seismic activity. To mitigate the potential for frost heaving, foundations should always extend below the regional frost depth. To further resist overturning and wind loads, mechanically tying the foundation to the masonry unit is recommended. Foundation data for piers is provided in Table 4.4. Foundations must also penetrate to frost depth or deeper. Frost depth information is provided on the following page. The depth of the foundation should be the *greater* of these two factors.

Table 4.4 Required Embedment for Pier Foundation. (Used with permission of the Brick Industry Association.)

Wall Span (ft)	Wind Load (10 psf)			Wind Load (15 psf)			Wind Load (20 psf)		
	Wall Height (ft)			Wall Height (ft)			Wall Height (ft)		
	4	*6*	*8*	*4*	*6*	*8*	*4*	*6*	*8*
8	2' 0"	2' 3"	2' 9"	2' 3"	2' 6"	3' 0"	2' 3"	2' 9"	3' 0"
10	2' 0"	2' 6"	2' 9"	2' 3"	2' 9"	3' 3"	2' 6"	3' 0"	3' 3"
12	2' 3"	2' 6"	3' 0"	2' 3"	3' 0"	3' 3"	2' 6"	3' 3"	3' 6"
14	2' 3"	2' 9"	3' 0"	2' 6"	3' 0"	3' 3"	2' 9"	3' 3"	3' 9"
16	2' 3"	2' 9"	3' 0"	2' 6"	3' 3"	3' 6"	2' 9"	3' 6"	4' 0"

Within shaded areas, 24 in. diameter foundation required. All other values obtained with 18 in. diameter foundation. (See fig 4.4)

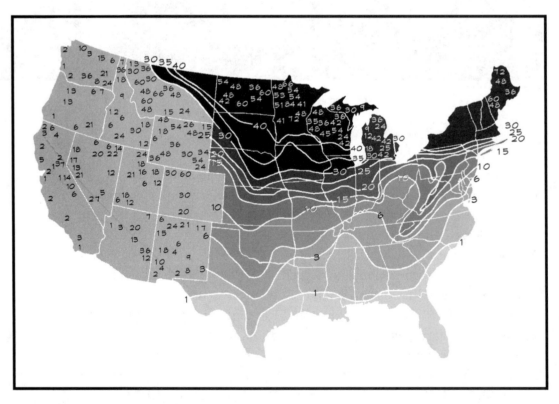

The average depth in inches of frost penetration in the United States. The depth of a foundation should be the greater of either frost penetration or structural requirements as indicated in Table 4.4.

THE BUSY DESIGNER'S QUICK REFERENCE GUIDE:
Columns, Piers, and Pilasters

- Columns and piers are freestanding masonry elements; pilasters are integrated into the wall itself.

- Columns serve primarily as vertical supports. Piers and pilasters must provide lateral support.

- Pier-and-panel walls use structural piers to support relatively thin brick wall panels that span from pier to pier.

- In a landscape, masonry columns provide adequate support for vertical loads. Piers and pilasters require additional reinforcing to resist lateral forces.

- Foundations must extend to recommended structural depths or to the local frost depth, whichever is greater.

- As in walls, the topmost surface of columns, piers, and pilasters must be capped for water resistance.

5

Brick sculptures express the beauty of brick through the hand of the artist. (Courtesy of Brickstone Studios.)

5
DESIGN
CONSIDERATIONS

BRICK FINISHES

TEXTURE

Currently, the majority of bricks are produced using the stiff-mud extrusion process, in which clay is forced through a die, imparting the profile of the brick. As the clay exits the die, or later in the conveyor sequence, a variety of textures and finishes may be imparted to the brick. As it is extruded, the clay is quite smooth. Different treatments may be used to score or roughen the surface for the desired texture. A very popular and common texture is the wire-cut, or velour, finish. Wires, set at the mouth of the die, remove extra material from the sides of the extruded clay, creating a rough texture. A rug finish yields a rough, mottled texture. Other familiar textures include stippled, striated, molded, matte, and smooth. As its name implies, a bark finish is a rough, scale-like finish reminiscent of a tree's bark. Manufacturers may also apply names to their own unique finishing processes, such as "rustic," "antique," and "torn." The designation "iron-spot" refers to the presence of small metallic fragments in the brick. These small flecks add distinct visual interest to a brick's finish. For designers, the best approach is to select a finish based on samples provided by the manufacturer or its representative.

In addition, the clay may be sprinkled with sand for a sand finish after it has been extruded. However, is not to be confused with bricks that are sand-*struck*. Bricks manufactured by the soft-mud process of molding may be sand-struck for a rough, gritty surface, or water-struck for a smoother one. Both measures also facilitate the removal of the clay from the mold used in the soft-mud process.

GLAZING

A glazed ceramic coating on one or more faces of a brick offers additional options of color and texture for designers. Glazes are fired to an impervious state in the kiln. The specific standards for glazed brick are governed by ASTM C126, Standard Specification for Ceramic Structural Clay Facing Tile, Facing Brick and Solid Masonry Units or C1405, Standard Specification for Glazed Brick (single fired, solid brick units). Today most glazes are sprayed on the clay prior to firing. The temperature generated during burning (1850°F to 2000°F) fuses the glaze to the brick. Glazed finishes range from glossy to matte and can result in a range of different colors. Certain colors that cannot be produced at these high temperatures are achieved by applications to the brick after firing. The treated brick is then conveyed back through the kiln and fired at lower temperatures. This is referred to as double-fired glazed brick.

Salt glazing is an older and less used method of glazing brick. It can be traced back several centuries and was used to create water-impervious surfaces on crockery as well as on bricks. A vapor of salt and chemicals is introduced into the kiln near the completion of the burning process. This forms a durable vitreous film that becomes integral to all exposed brick surfaces. The familiar glazed brick headers seen in colonial architecture are salt glazed.

Glazed brick offers yet another finish option for designers, but it is not recommended for paving situations owing to its inherent lack of traction. Landscape designers must take extra care when proposing glazed brick. In certain applications the water-impervious glazing surface actually traps internal moisture and prevents it from evaporating, possibly promoting water damage. The specific detail must be designed with special care to prevent opportunities for water intrusion into a wall system, especially one that calls for bricks faced with a glazed finish. Glazed bricks are recommended for use in vented cavity walls only.

THE BUSY DESIGNER'S QUICK REFERENCE GUIDE:
Brick Finishes

- In the stiff-mud process, brick finishes are applied as the brick is extruded.
- The wire-cut, or velour, finish is achieved as extruded brick is sliced into individual units by a wire cutting tool.
- Other popular finishes include rug, stippled, striated, molded, sand, smooth, and bark.
- Iron-spot refers to small metallic fragments imbedded in the clay.
- Manufacturers may offer unique finishes of their own design.
- Soft-mud processed brick may be sand-struck or water-struck.
- Glazing imparts an impervious, smooth coating, available in a range of colors and gloss onto a brick's face.
- Glazing may curtail the venting of moisture from brick.
- Glazed brick is inappropriate for use in pavements.

BONDS AND BONDING

Although the visual effects of bonding are important design considerations, the primary purpose of bonding is structural. Designers are prone to consider bonding as a visual pattern alone, failing to recognize the structural role of bonds in a wall. Patterns may result from the different bonds, but are not their source. Bonding is a careful balancing act of form and function. Imagine a wall composed entirely of stretchers arranged in a stack bond. All vertical joints would extend the full height of the wall, and there would be no link between wythes, unless by mechanical means. Without the bonding of bricks within a wall, any structural load would be transferred vertically down a single column of bricks. Such a wall would be no stronger than the mortar joints holding the individual columns of bricks together. Bonding yields greater strength as it transfers the load diagonally along the interwoven pattern of either half- or quarter-brick overlaps.

In a double-wythe exterior wall it is important to join the wythes with either a header brick or metal ties. The decision is based purely on visual considerations, as these methods perform equally well in bonding the wythes to one another. Turned 90 degrees to the face of the wall in order to span both

Anatomy of bonding. This cutaway view reveals the course-by-course configuration of a common bond wall with a bonding course of headers at every sixth row. Note the use of half-width queen closures at the corners to maintain staggered joints.

wythes, the header brick is so named because it exposes its header face instead of its stretcher face.

The various compositions that may be achieved with combinations of headers and stretchers gives rise to increased opportunities for visual interest and are the genesis of common, English, Flemish, and Dutch bonds. Brick walls in a landscape typically differ from architectural walls in one important aspect. A freestanding (nonretaining) exterior wall must provide two fair faces, whereas an architectural wall requires only one. Both faces of an exterior wall must be kept straight, which is difficult owing to the variability of brick lengths. The designer should give careful attention to the selection of a bond pattern. Too often this decision is based purely on the visual characteristics of a particular bond pattern. Yet the various bonds differ in internal strength and stability. A simple guideline in considering the strength of a bond (or a paving pattern, for that matter) is to minimize long, unbroken linear joints, especially in the vertical orientation. A stack bond has vertical joints that run the entire height of the wall, both on the exterior face and internally. This is the weakest bond of any. There is, in fact, no "bond" at all in this bond! (i.e., there are no masonry units that work to tie the wall into a unified, interwoven unit). Horizontal joint reinforcement would be necessary to tie (bond) the wythes of such a wall.

RUNNING BOND

A running bond wall offers visual simplicity (or monotony, depending on the designer's point of view). It is composed entirely of stretchers placed in half-lap or third-lap alignments. Without header bricks, the running bond lacks the ability to bind its wythes. A double-wythe wall incorporating only a running bond requires the introduction of mechanical bonds to unite the wythes. Otherwise, the lack of binding between the wythes would result in their eventual separation.

ENGLISH BOND

The English bond, with its alternating courses of stretchers and headers, yields an extraordinarily strong wall. No "straight joints" (any joint common to two adjoining courses) extend vertically along either its face or depth. If one could dismantle such a wall, no internal straight vertical joints would be found within the wall. It is this high degree of interlocking that gives the English bond its tremendous strength. Each lap is a quarter-bond, and a special "closer brick" (a brick that is half the width of a header) is required at the wall's ends and corners (quoins) to maintain the pattern of quarter-laps. Without the closer brick, the two headers sitting atop one stretcher at a 90 degree corner would result in an undesirable straight vertical joint that would repeat along the wall's face. Often three or five courses of stretchers are placed between header courses for economy, but the resulting internal straight joints will naturally yield a wall of somewhat diminished strength.

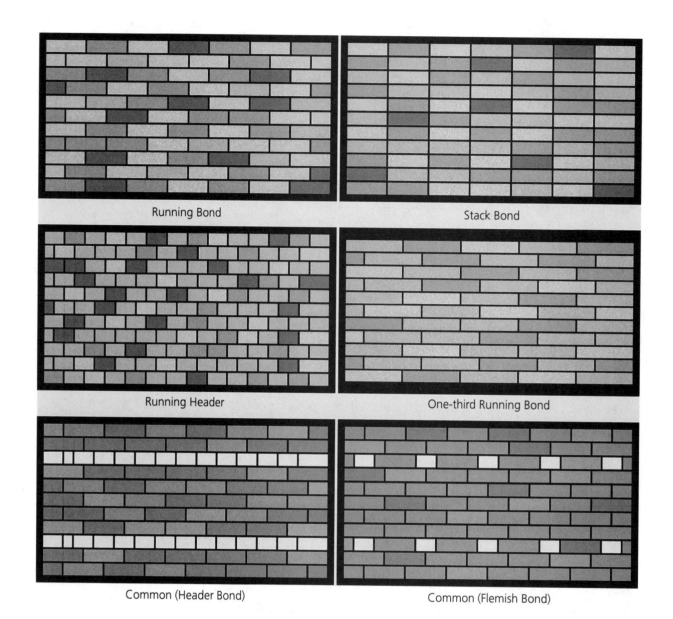

Running Bond

Stack Bond

Running Header

One-third Running Bond

Common (Header Bond)

Common (Flemish Bond)

A portfolio of brick bonds.

FLEMISH BOND

Whereas the English bond alternates header courses and stretcher courses of brick, the Flemish bond alternates header bricks and stretcher bricks in *each* course. Like the English bond, it features quarter-laps exclusively and requires closer bricks at corners and ends to maintain the strength and to avoid straight joints. The header bricks in each course may be separated by three stretchers bricks instead of one for simplicity.

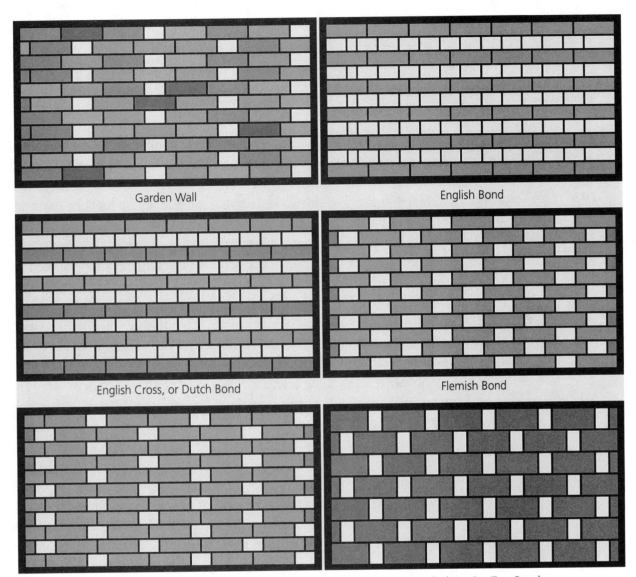

Garden Wall

English Bond

English Cross, or Dutch Bond

Flemish Bond

Flemish, Double Stretcher

Rowlock, or Rat Trap Bond

DUTCH BOND

The Dutch bond is really a variation of the English bond. It is similar in appearance, but substitutes ¾ bats at the corners in place of the closer bricks required in the English bond.

COMMON BOND

The common bond is essentially a running bond, but it incorporates headers at every fifth, sixth, or seventh course to serve as ties between wythes.

The header course may be continuous, as in an English bond, or alternating between stretchers as in a Flemish bond. The common bond is sometimes referred to as the American bond.

SOLDIER COURSING

Soldier courses can add visual interest to any bond pattern, creating visual bands at key locations in the wall. A soldier course is achieved by turning stretchers on end, resembling a row of soldiers standing at attention. Although this is a simple and effective technique, it also harbors a number of pitfalls that designers must anticipate and resolve. An area of special concern is where a soldier course must turn a 90 degree corner. Most bricks have finished stretcher and header faces, because these are commonly exposed on walls. Often, however, the bricks have unfinished shiner faces, and worse, this face is frequently cored. Few details do more to detract from a design more than exposed core holes that are subsequently filled with mortar. Although more subtle, unfinished exposed faces at corners of soldier courses also reveal a lack of sophistication in detailing.

Rather than avoiding soldier courses in walls altogether, designers have three methods to mitigate this problem. The simplest solution is to ensure that a number of standard, uncored bricks with identically finished shiner faces are ordered with the face bricks. For a more sophisticated detail, designers can order special bricks that are square in section, offering two identically finished exterior faces. A third option is the installation of mitered brick at the corners, which places a vertical mortar joint at the corner.

Another potential problem is the use of brick whose soldier course height is not an even multiple of three stretcher courses, which results in the need to cut and install a thin stretcher course to accommodate the difference. This solution is costly, unattractive, and more prone to damage owing to the thinness of the bricks. Standard bricks have an actual length of 8 in. and a stretcher height of 2¼ in. Adding the dimensions of three stretchers plus two ⅜ in. mortar joints yields a total dimension of 7½ in., measured from the bottom brick face to the top, a full ½ in. shorter than its 8 in. soldier course height. Modular bricks, whose actual length averages 7⅝ in., match the multiple of three standard brick stretcher courses. Designers using standard 8 inch units must remember to specify the proper quantity of modular bricks to accommodate any soldier coursing called for in the design.

THE BUSY DESIGNER'S QUICK REFERENCE GUIDE:
Bonds and Bonding

- Although it creates opportunities for visual interest, the primary function of bonding is structural.
- Bonding ties multiple wythes together and distributes vertical loads diagonally.
- Bonding is most commonly achieved with headers.
- Mechanical ties may be used when bond patterns do not include headers.
- Popular bonds include the stack bond, running bond, common bond, English bond, Flemish bond, Dutch bond, and garden wall.
- The rowlock, or rat-trap, bond utilizes rowlock stretchers in lieu of stretchers.
- Soldier courses are commonly used to add interest, especially at a wall's cap.

JOINT DESIGN

The total area of mortared joints in a typical brick wall comprises approximately 17% of its surface. Simply put, the role of mortared joints is to bind the individual brick units into a structurally sound unit. From a designer's perspective, however, the joints serve other functions beyond adhesion. In both vertical and horizontal applications, brick joints serve at least two other primary purposes. Studies reveal that the overwhelming majority of masonry failures occur at the joints. The mortar joints in a brick installation must provide effective protection from the forces of weather, especially water resistance, inasmuch as standing water is particularly detrimental to brick construction. In addition, the depth and profile of mortar joints have an important role in the overall visual appearance of a wall. The joint design in a skillfully crafted masonry installation represents a balancing of form and function that must accomplish both of these ends equally well.

To achieve resistance to weather, a well-tooled joint must prevent water from remaining in the joint. Given adequate time, water can work its way into a joint and ultimately degrade the bond between the mortar and the masonry unit. Once this bond is defeated, a cycle of failure ensues. In cold climates, freezing action on any standing moisture hastens the failure of the

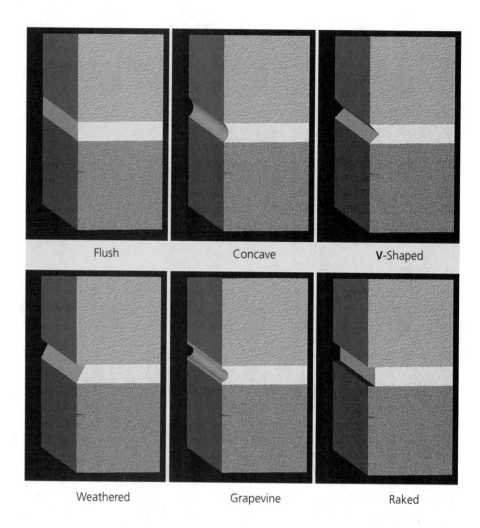

Flush   Concave   **V**-Shaped

Weathered   Grapevine   Raked

Typical mortar joints.

joint. Unsightly efflorescence is another problem promoted by the intrusion of water into a masonry wall. Water absorbs the salts and soluble compounds found in both brick and mortar, resulting in a familiar white stain on the surface. Efflorescence is more a symptom than a problem in and of itself. Those dreaded white stains are good indicators that water is present within the wall, probably doing greater damage than just discoloring the surface.

In joint design and selection, it follows that any joint providing a horizontal "shelf" on which water may stand for a period of time is unacceptable. From a weathering perspective and for the strongest bonding, concave, **V**-shaped, or struck (weathered) tooled joints are the best options. Concave, **V**, and weathered joints provide more visual interest and depth than flush joints, while providing excellent moisture resistance. Water drains quickly from these joint profiles because they offer no flat surface on which moisture may collect and sit. Beaded and grapevine joints are also considered acceptable, provided that the point at which the mortar meets the brick is essentially a flush condition. These provide no horizontal surfaces for water to remain and offer no recesses for water intrusion. Flush joints also prevent water from entering a joint, but they are not tooled to an effective degree of compaction during their installation and thus result in a somewhat less dense surface. Further, the process of finishing a flush joint can actually draw off a small quantity of the mortar's surface, exposing the less compressed interior. And although a flush joint provides the maximal bearing for each individual brick, it does not bond as well to the brick units as do tooled joints. From a visual perspective, the severe flatness of a flush joint can be somewhat limiting. Designers often desire the shadows, depth, and visual interest that result from more deeply tooled joints.

The potential for water penetration into joints can also be discouraged in other ways. A well-tooled joint both smoothes and compacts the mortar into the joint, providing greater water resistance. Certain joints such as struck and raked joints actually encourage water intrusion by providing a flat surface at the bottom of the joint on which water may sit indefinitely. These joints are only marginally suitable for exterior brick walls. If used, they must be carefully and smoothly tooled, diminishing any irregularities or roughness that permits water retention.

The so-called extruded or weeping joint, in which mortar appears to ooze from a wall's surface, provides plentiful opportunity for water to remain in contact with both the joint and the surface of the brick. The visual interest of this type of joint is primarily a novelty, and its resistance to the weather is extremely poor. Given their lengthy training and skill, experienced masons consider this joint as little more than poor workmanship. This profile is unacceptable for almost any exterior application.

The variety of joint types, along with the spectrum of mortar colors, provides the designer a wide range of design options. Joints may be either emphasized or deemphasized, depending on the designer's preference, by varying their width, profile, depth, and color. The innovative architect Frank Lloyd Wright recognized the visual opportunities presented by mortar joints. He typically specified deeply raked horizontal joints combined with flush vertical joints to emphasize the strong horizontal lines of his buildings. He also recommended coloring the vertical joints to closely match the hue of the surrounding brick, further denying the vertical joints in contrast to the vividly expressed horizontal joints.

The extruded or weeping joint creates opportunities for water to remain in extended contact with the joints. Its value is primarily as a novelty, but it represents questionable detailing.

THE BUSY DESIGNER'S QUICK REFERENCE GUIDE:
Joint Design

- In a brick wall the joints account for approximately 17% of the visible surface.

- The primary purpose of mortar joints is adhesion.

- Most masonry failure occurs at the joints.

- Joints must also provide weather resistance and serve an important visual function in a wall.

- A sound joint eliminates opportunities for water to remain at any location where the mortar meets a brick.

- The process of tooling a joint serves to compress the mortar, enhancing its water-resistant capacity.

- Concave, **V**, and weathered joints are the best types to use when water intrusion is a concern.

- Flush joints offer an effective profile to resist water, but are not tooled to a suitable compression during installation.

- Colored mortar is widely available.

SPECIAL TECHNIQUES

By its very nature, brick is a rich and visually pleasing construction material. Its small unit size permits a great deal of variation within a large surface. To get the most from brick, designers should be familiar with techniques beyond flush surfaces and the running bond. Although brick excels at quietly blending into a landscape, it can also capture the spotlight when designers take full advantage of its unique properties to create surface patterning, depth, and shadowing. There are a number of time-honored methods of enhancing a brick installation to achieve added interest. Bricklayers are trained and eager to install more advanced brickwork, but designers request it all too infrequently.

The flexibility and small unit size of brick make possible an unlimited range of unique expressions in brickwork.

DIAPERING

Diapers are the various diagonal and diamond-shaped patterns created by inserting contrasting brick colors into certain bonds. The stretcher and header combinations in variations of the Flemish and Dutch bonds are particularly adaptable to the creation of diapers. The degree of contrast between a diaper's figure and its field will determine the liveliness of the pattern.

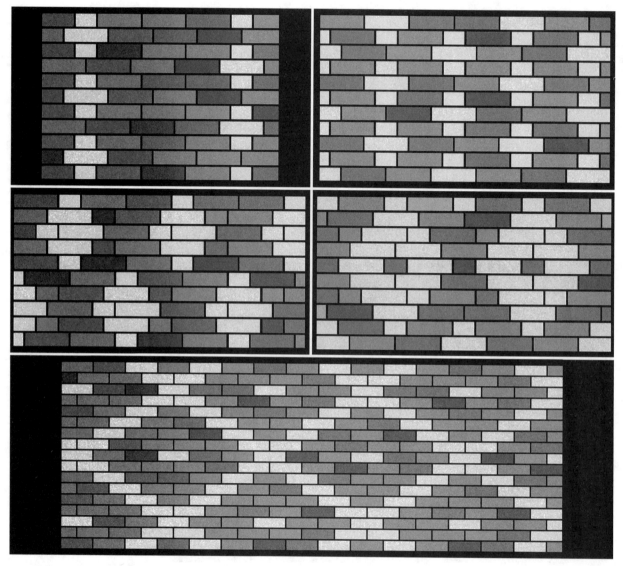

Using bricks of contrasting colors, the various bonds employed in brickwork can yield a surprising range of diapering patterns.

CORBELING

Corbeling is the projecting or cantilevering of one brick, or a course of bricks, beyond the course directly beneath it. It appears as a reverse stair-stepping effect. The structural requirements for corbeling are simple, but must be closely adhered to.

1. The total corbeled projection should not exceed one-half the total thickness of the wall.

2. No individual corbeled projection should exceed one-third the dimension of a single wythe.
3. No individual corbeled projection should exceed one-half the nominal brick height.

These guidelines serve to ensure the stability of the entire wall, as well as to prevent damage to the corbeled bricks, whose tensile strength is increased with the surcharge of the cantilevered load stacked above them.

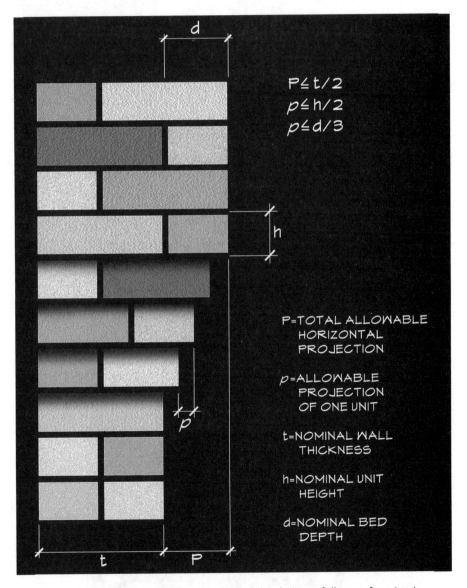

$$P \leq t/2$$
$$p \leq h/2$$
$$p \leq d/3$$

P=TOTAL ALLOWABLE HORIZONTAL PROJECTION

p=ALLOWABLE PROJECTION OF ONE UNIT

t=NOMINAL WALL THICKNESS

h=NOMINAL UNIT HEIGHT

d=NOMINAL BED DEPTH

Corbels can create depth and shadow, provided the designer follows a few simple structural guidelines.

QUOINS

Brick and stone quoins provide the designer with an effective means of adding visual interest and strength where a wall turns or terminates. Quoins of contrasting or matching brick can be installed without the added cost or complexity of introducing additional materials, such as stone or precast concrete. Quoins can be projected from the face of a wall as a form of rusticated brickwork (see below) and are usually installed at the ends or corners of walls. Quoins may also be flush with the wall's face, appearing only as a contrasting color or pattern. Traditionally, quoins are five courses in height, although they frequently vary between three and seven courses to fit proportionally within the wall's overall height. Quoins may project up to 1³⁄₁₆ in. (using standard modular brick) from the face of the wall. As with corbels, the projection should not exceed one-third the depth of the wythe. Quoins are normally sep-

Quoins may be made from brick or other compatible masonry materials.

arated vertically by one or more flush courses. It is most efficient to restrict the horizontal length of a quoin to a 4 in. module. The designer has the option of varying the ratio of flush to projected courses, and of varying the length of the quoin along the wall's face. An interesting visual effect is achieved by alternating longer and shorter quoins vertically along a wall's corner.

Flush quoins, although often constructed by varying the masonry material, may also be created by using brick of a contrasting color. Simpler to construct than projecting quoins, they result in a relatively minor cost increase to the masonry budget, inasmuch as a smaller quantity of the contrasting brick must be ordered and the mason will sort the brick and cut the half-bricks as they are installed. The half-bricks typically used to terminate the quoins result in nearly continuous vertical joints, ideal locations for expansion joints.

In using cored brick to construct projecting quoins or corbels, care must be taken to prevent exposing the holes and creating the opportunity for water

Quoins of a contrasting brick create visual interest while adding only moderately to the overall cost.

penetration. Most specifications allow cores within ¾ in. of a brick's edge. The arrangement of core patterns is at the discretion of the manufacturer and will vary significantly. Designers must become familiar with the specific brick being supplied and must accommodate the dimension between a brick's face and its nearest cored holes when determining the projection of a quoin or a corbel.

DOG'S TOOTH

The dog's tooth method is often used for a course or an infill panel within a more traditional bond. To achieve the "tooth," a header is turned 45 degrees to the face of the wall. It is especially critical that the exposed corners are carefully aligned vertically. For bonding strength, the bricks in the dog's toothed panel should alternate orientation with each course.

The 45-degree-angled dog's tooth course adds to the composition of this ornate brick wall.

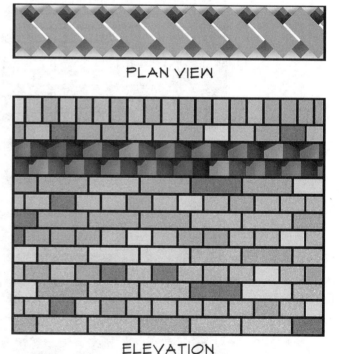

PLAN VIEW

ELEVATION

Creating dog's tooth coursing is quite simple, as revealed in this plan and elevation.

Simple skintling imparts a rustic, casual feel to brick masonry.

Although less common, skintling can be geometric and patterned rather than random.

SKINTLING

You might test the mettle of your brick mason by using this relatively obscure term. In its simplest form, *skintling* is the canting of a brick so that one corner protrudes, usually slightly, from a true vertical alignment. Skintling can be random, as shown above, yielding a quaint, rustic cottage look, or it can be patterned and rhythmic as illustrated below. In this example one-fourth of the length of each stretcher is corbeled above the course below. The *back* corner of each successive brick in a course is aligned with the *center* of the header of the preceding brick. The fifth brick course aligns vertically directly above the first course. Each ascending course is also recessed slightly to maintain the alignment of each projecting corner along the same vertical plane. Although seeming to defy gravity, each skintled brick is amply supported along approximately 80% of its base, and support beneath opposite corners further stabilizes the technique.

RUSTICATED BRICKWORK

Rusticated masonry is typified by distinct recesses between individual masonry units or, as with brick, between multiple courses of masonry units. Rustication is thought to add a perceived visual strength to a masonry wall. It was an essential component in classical Greek and Roman architecture, usually applied to the lowest level of a building, where a sense of visual strength is most critical. In brick applications, the indentations are typically placed every sixth course. Further visual contrast can be achieved by composing the recessed brick course entirely of headers or rowlocks. For the

Rustication bestows a visual strength to brickwork.

optimum visual resolution, the designer should take care to ensure that a rusticated course occurs at the bottom and top courses, dictating a wall height that is an even multiple of six courses plus the single additional rusticated course. Chamfered brick, placed above and below each recessed course, can add to the overall effect of rustication while discouraging the accumulation of water, snow, or ice.

SERPENTINE WALLS

Serpentine walls were constructed long before Thomas Jefferson's well-known installation on the campus of the University of Virginia in the early part of the nineteenth century. Serpentine walls may, in fact, predate written history. The structural qualities of a single-wythe serpentine wall are similar to those of corrugated materials. Their inherent strength is a result of their opposing curvatures, which eliminate the need for supporting piers at periodic intervals.

Thomas Jefferson's well-known serpentine brick wall at the University of Virginia exhibits a graceful meandering form while capitalizing on its structural benefits.

Serpentine walls can also enhance city landscapes.

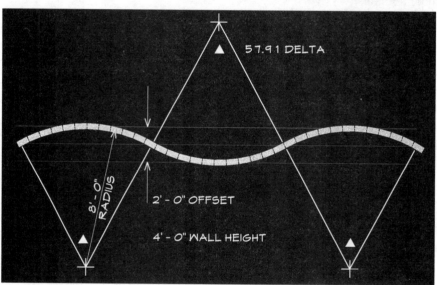

57.91 DELTA

8' - 0" RADIUS

2' - 0" OFFSET

4' - 0" WALL HEIGHT

The layout geometry for serpentine walls.

For minor exterior serpentine walls (walls 4 ft in height or less) the mathematics of corrugation are fairly simple. Containing no tangents between the reverse curves, the radii should not exceed twice the overall height of the wall, or 8 ft for a 4 ft high wall. The corresponding depth of curvature (the total horizontal offset) should not be less than one-half the height, or 2 ft for the same 4 ft high wall. A structural analysis should be conducted for walls taller than 4 ft (see Table 5.1).

Table 5.1 Centerline Geometry for Serpentine Walls.

Height of Wall	Radius	Depth of Curve	Length of Curve	r
3' 0"	6' 0"	1' 6"	6' ¾"	57.91°
3' 6"	7' 0"	1' 9"	7' ⅞"	57.91°
4' 0"	8' 0"	2' 0"	8' 1"	57.91°

SCULPTED BRICK

Sculpted, or carved, brickwork is making a comeback. This product, the result of an artistic yet labor-intensive process of shaping individual bricks prior to firing, is a close relative of terra-cotta. Both were largely eschewed during the Modern movement, seen as needlessly ornamental and costly. The

Sculpting brick while still green adds another dimension to its range of uses in a landscape.

A portfolio of brick sculptures.
(Top 3 photos courtesy of
Brickstone Studios.)

current revival is being championed by artists more than craftsworkers, with sculpted brickworks viewed more as objects of art than as integral building components. It is somewhat misleading to simply categorize sculpted brick as expensive masonry. From a design perspective, sculpted brick actually represents an economical way to produce hand-made sculpture as compared with hand-sculpted stone or metal constructions. And brick sculpture satisfies the "one percent for art" where required on government construction projects.

In a landscape, sculpted brick offers the added benefit of harmonizing visually with other brick elements in the composition. There are three general methods of producing sculpted brick pieces. The most common method is intaglio, a process in which the design is incised into the face of unfired standard brick. When a sculpture with more relief is desired, green brick with a thickness greater than the standard modular 3⅝ in. is used for carving. This bas-relief method allows the sculpture to both *recede into* and *project from* the adjacent wall surface. In both methods, the sculpted brick is assembled into a panel while still green, so its production requires considerably less effort than the carving or chiseling of stone. Following the sculpting process, the individual bricks are coded according to their course and their position within that course, much like being assigned to columns and rows. After the panel is disassembled, the bricks are kiln-fired and reassembled on-site. A third method of creating sculpted brick pieces involves cutting the brick after it is fired, usually on-site, then assembling it into the final sculpture.

When a solid, monolithic appearance is desired, the mortar may be color matched to the general hue of the bricks, and the joints flush-struck. Some artists prefer to celebrate individual bricks over the whole assembly, however. There is a bit of irony in using such a relatively small and commonplace material to achieve what are often monumental and elegant works of art. Many artists choose to call attention to, rather than deny, the individual bricks that constitute their works, highlighting the joints by using mortar of a contrasting color or by striking joints with deeper and more noticeable profiles.

COMMON PROBLEMS

It is not the intent of this book to instruct designers on methods for the repair of deteriorated brick installations. Certain masonry problems are clearly beyond the influence of the designer, such as those that result from defective

THE BUSY DESIGNER'S QUICK REFERENCE GUIDE:
Special Techniques

- Diapers are diagonal and diamond-shaped patterns in brickwork.
- Corbeling refers to bricks that project from a wall's surface.
- Quoins are patterns of either projecting or contrasting bricks at the corners or ends of a brick wall.
- Projected quoins must adhere to the rules that govern sound corbeling.
- Dog's tooth is a process wherein bricks are rotated 45 degrees relative to a wall's surface.
- Skintling is the canting of a brick so that one corner protrudes from the flush face.
- A rusticated wall features recessed courses, usually at regular intervals.
- Serpentine walls add visual interest while gaining added strength from their curving geometry.
- Sculpted brick is most often created prior to its firing.
- The most common method of sculpting brick is the intaglio process.

material that fails to meet standards of the American Society for Testing and Materials (ASTM). Still other failures may result from poor workmanship during installation. A poorly tooled joint and the presence of mortar droppings in a drainage wall are common sources of problems. And nothing constructed by humans is completely maintenance-free. Problems can occur in masonry that is simply neglected.

Designers are rarely without fault or obligation, however. Many common problems can be traced directly to poor detailing, and an ounce of prevention during the design phase is worth a pound of cure later. There are a number of forces that can work to deteriorate all forms of masonry construction, including brick. Among the most widespread design-related problems are those that arise from the failure to adequately protect brick installations from extended exposure to moisture. But water is not the only enemy of masonry. The list of forces present in the exterior environment that can deteriorate brick masonry is, unfortunately, a long one. Designers must be constantly wary of details and configurations that can ultimately compromise the masonry's performance. Preparing a good, sound detail is half the battle.

WHY BRICKS DETERIORATE

Bricks begin life as soft clay. Despite the partial ceramic vitrification that occurs during firing at high temperatures, bricks are susceptible to rapid or gradual deterioration under the right combination of stresses. Especially true in the built landscape is the undeniable reality that nature relentlessly strives to reclaim materials through a process of erosion, degradation, and deterioration. The realistic goal is to retard this process of reclamation to a practical minimum, not to eliminate it entirely. There are a number of forces that can ultimately lead to damaged bricks or failed mortar joints, which can be grouped in five broad categories:

Physical stress (settling, structural movement, restricted expansion)
Hydric activity (water intrusion, freeze-and-thaw cycles)
Geological movement (Soil expansion and seismic activity)
Chemical exposure (pollution and acid rain)
Biological activity (climbing vegetation and fungi)

Notice that normal weathering is not included in this list. No material or construction is intended to last indefinitely, utterly unchanged. In fact, the grace with which brick weathers is one of its strongest design attributes. Designers should be concerned with those stresses that serve to *accelerate* natural weathering. Although these forces may be more or less ever-present, depending on regional conditions, their effects can be greatly magnified by poor detailing, defective material, or substandard workmanship.

EFFLORESCENCE

Efflorescence is the all-too-familiar whitish discoloration on the surface of finished masonry. It is caused by the deposition of soluble salts as water evaporates from the masonry unit. Yet although it is visually troublesome, as mentioned earlier, efflorescence is more a symptom than a problem itself. It is a reliable indicator that unwanted water has penetrated the installation. The finger of blame is often pointed at the brick or mortar itself, but soluble salts are normally present in masonry units and other adjacent materials. Their mere presence is not a conclusive indication of defective manufacturing. The only effective solution lies in finding the source of the water penetration and rerouting or eliminating it. This will prevent further efflorescence from forming, but will not eliminate the existing stains. Although good design is critical to the *prevention* of efflorescence, designers are not typically called upon to help determine a means of removing it. A table of effective cleaning agents and step-by-step methods for their application and the treatment of such stains can be found in *Cleaning Masonry: A Review of the Literature,* by Clayford T. Grimm.

SPALLING

Spalling is the flaking away, or exfoliating, of a brick's outer surface. The pressure of expanding ice in an already saturated brick can cause the brick to spall. In extruded brick, this tends to occur along its lamination planes. The pressure exerted by expanding soluble salts and freeze-and-thaw cycles are other common catalysts of spalling. Older, softer brick may be damaged when mortar repairs utilize incompatible mortar. Modern mortar mixes are measurably harder than older lime-based mortars, and the force they exert on older brick can lead to its spalling or cracking. Spalled brick cannot be repaired but must be removed and replaced. The most effective means of preventing spalling is to ensure that materials meet all applicable standards and that the masonry remains relatively dry.

CRACKING

It is not particularly difficult to crack a brick. Like most masonry units, brick is extremely strong in compression but relatively weak in tension. The martial artist who snaps a brick in two is taking advantage of this characteristic tensile weakness. Although capable of supporting great loads, a poorly designed brick installation that exerts even moderate tensile forces on a brick can result in its cracking. Cracks are often found when brick is used in spanning situations, above openings such as gates, arches, doors, and windows. If the support beneath the brick is underdesigned and permitted to deflect, the structural load of the brick above the spanning course exerts tensile force on it. Corbeling a brick beyond a third of its wythe or half of its nominal height also places it under similar stress that can lead to its cracking.

Cracked brick in rigid paving situations may result from inadequately designed expansion joints. If the matrix of brick and mortar expands without relief, stress will build up within the pavement system. Without the safety valve provided by expansion joints, these forces will invariably find the weakest point in the matrix, often relieving the stress by cracking bricks and/or mortar joints. Cracking may also result from the differential expansion or movement of rigid base materials, particularly concrete, on which the pavers are installed. When existing site conditions prevent the introduction of adequately spaced expansion joints, a bond-break installed between the brick and the rigid base permits differential movement. Cracking is far less likely to occur in flexible (nonmortared) brick pavements. These systems offer greater opportunities to distribute and relieve the stresses of movement and expansion.

The individual hairline cracking of a single brick is not catastrophic, provided the structural condition has achieved equilibrium and further movement is stabilized. If the cracked unit(s) cannot be replaced, simply sealing the crack to prevent the potential of water intrusion will suffice. Cracks that are longer, with openings wide enough for water penetration, are symptomatic of serious structural flaws, however, and require significant repairs.

Armed with an understanding of the most common masonry problems, designers can better undertake mitigating measures during the detailing phase. Foundations that extend fully to frost depth minimize the opportunity for movement resulting from freeze-and-thaw cycles. The installation of

---

THE BUSY DESIGNER'S QUICK REFERENCE GUIDE:
Common Problems

- Problems can arise from faulty manufacturing, installation, and/or design.

- General deterioration is a natural process of reclamation. Skillful design will retard this process to a practical minimum.

- Deteriorating stresses fall into five broad categories: physical stress, hydric activity, geological movement, chemical exposure, and biological activity.

- Efflorescence is a whitish discoloration of masonry caused by soluble salts.

- Efflorescence is a symptom of unvented or undrained water in masonry construction.

- Spalling is the flaking away of a brick's outer surface.

- Cracking is usually caused when brick is subjected to excessive tensile stress.

properly sized and sloped copings of either stone or specially molded brick, with adequate overhangs and drip edges, provides critical water repelling capabilities in a masonry wall. Joint profile should also be considered as a design issue. Certain profiles such as concave, **V**, or weathered joints to a better job of preventing water from remaining in a mortar joint. Other profiles may actually encourage water retention by providing recesses or horizontal surfaces. Rigid pavements require properly spaced, watertight expansion joints that extend through each rigid layer. Weep holes in cavity and retaining walls are necessary to facilitate the removal of water from locations where it can damage brickwork. Making these issues primary considerations during the design phase will minimize problems and slow deterioration throughout the life of a project.

ENVIRONMENTAL ISSUES

Simple brick represents a complex issue when its environmental friendliness is evaluated. Every aspect of the construction trade is coming under increased scrutiny relative to its environmental performance. Certainly, the designer bears a significant responsibility in the selection of materials, overall site configuration, and the degree of on-site cutting and waste. The environmental characteristics of any building material, including brick, must be measured during every step of its life-cycle. The potential for environmental impacts arises during its mining and production, its transportation, its installation, its in-place performance, and during its eventual disposal and/or recycling.

The extraction of the clay or shale—a mined natural resource—of which brick is composed carries undeniable environmental impact. Fortunately, clay is relatively abundant throughout the world. Most clay is surface mined and processed locally, minimizing the energy used to transport it to the kiln. Clays with greater purity that are used for specialized purposes, such as fire brick, come from deeper in the earth, however, and accessing them carries greater economic and environmental costs. The reclaiming of clay mines when operations cease is required by the Environmental Protection Agency (EPA).

One of the most significant environmental issues relative to brick production arises from its need for high-temperature burning for extended periods. A temperature of 2100°F (1149°C) is generated for the partial vitrification of clay, which is somewhat lower than the temperature required to produce cement for concrete. In addition, the drying of clay prior to firing requires up to 48 hours at temperatures between 100°F (38°C) and 400°F (204°C). Conscientiously managed (and economical) brick operations typically take advantage of waste heat from the kiln to dry their unfired bricks. Currently, most kilns rely on natural gas as their fuel, with coal and sawdust constituting a smaller percentage. The flow of natural gas can be regulated more precisely than fueling with coal, with significantly reduced sulfur dioxide emissions. Continued advancements in heat recapture promise to further reduce the volume of natural gas required for the burning of brick. Modern, computer-operated tunnel kilns have significantly enhanced the efficiency and safety of the brick burning process.

The potential for other mitigating measures lies in the composition of the brick itself. Ever since straw and dung were first added to clay to improve its stability while baking in the sun, the composition of brick clay has been continually evaluated and improved. The Brick Industry Association reports that current research is directed toward identifying additives that will both enhance brick quality and lower the temperature required to achieve vitrification during the firing process. A number of waste materials and by-products have been combined with clay, enhancing various characteristics of the finished brick. Although some of these additives may be hazardous in their raw state, the high temperatures used during brick production often encapsulate and neutralize their dangerous components.

The glazes used to finish brick represent another potential area of concern, although glazed brick constitutes only about 1% of all brick manufactured in the United States. Currently, most glazing is applied prior to burning and the extreme heat neutralizes its volatility. Its potential to off-gas is eliminated as the glazing becomes integral to the brick's surface. The larger environmental concern associated with glazes has to do with their storage, application, and disposal at the brick manufacturing facility.

Brick remains essentially stable during the construction phase and poses few environmental hazards. The on-site cutting of brick with a dry masonry saw can release silica dust into the air. The health hazards of dust can be nearly eliminated by using a wet saw that limits airborne particles while keeping the cutting blade cool. Mortar mixing and the washing of mixing equipment are also practices that can introduce pollutants into the air and ground. Mortarless, flexible pavements obviously eliminate this potential, but careful job-site practices are required for mortared masonry construction.

Although portable and convenient, this dry saw can create airborne pollutants that pose a health hazard.

Mortar that is delivered to the job site ready-mixed eliminates the hazard of airborne dust. Cleaners used to remove mortar and efflorescence from face brick may also contain chemicals that are hazardous to the environment. Care must be taken in handling and disposal to prevent their introduction into surface water, ground water or waste water systems.

As discussed earlier, most brick manufactured in the world is still mined, fired, and transported within a fairly localized region. Given the high cost of handling and shipping heavy pallets of brick long distances, even large national suppliers own and operate local clay mines throughout the country. And unlike stone masonry such as granite and marble, high-quality clay is abundant over a wide geographical area, rendering importation practically unnecessary. It remains both economically and environmentally responsible to minimize the transport of brick. As a result, the quantity of brick either imported or exported internationally is negligible.

In the majority of landscape applications, the specific thermal properties of brick have little impact on heating, ventilating, or air-conditioning costs. As a wind or sun screen, brick can certainly shelter buildings and outdoor spaces from unwanted chilling wind or from solar gain, but not measurably more than any other solid material placed in the same configuration.

Current efforts are under way to establish definitive standards for the environmental performance of construction materials and practices. The ASTM has created a "Green Buildings Subcommittee," whose mission is the development of environmental performance standards. The cost of managing landfills continues to push recycling to the forefront of environmental research, and construction materials are no exception. In demolition, non-mortared flexible paving systems require less energy, create less airborne dust, and result in a greater quantity of reusable bricks than rigid systems.

THE BUSY DESIGNER'S QUICK REFERENCE GUIDE:
Environmental Issues

- A designer's chosen building material, brick or otherwise, entails a certain degree of environmental impact during its extraction, processing, transport, installation, on-site environmental performance, and its ultimate disposal.
- The reclamation of clay mining sites is now an industry requirement.
- Bricks are fired in increasingly efficient kilns, with greater control of fuel resources.
- Clay is usually mined locally, minimizing the need for long-distance transport.
- Thoughtful design can minimize the need for on-site cutting and the production of waste material during installation.

A DESIGNER'S GUIDE TO ESTIMATING BRICK QUANTITIES

Estimating the quantity of brick needed for a project is easier than it may appear. The key to accurate estimating lies in the modular nature of brick, which is based on 4 in. increments. Despite the fact that brick is available in a variety of sizes, all modular brick can be configured in fractions or multiples of 4 in., measured to the center of the joints. The nominal length of a modular brick, 8 in., equals the sum of its specified length plus a single mortar joint, and is a multiple of 4 in. Three stretcher courses plus mortar joints also equals 8 in. In addition, all modular brick is either 4 in., 6 in., or 8 in. thick (nominally).

Masons and bricklayers routinely work with the principle of modularity. Rather than getting bogged down with the brick's specified dimensions, which entail clumsy fractions, or actual dimensions, which vary from brick to brick, designers should simply use the 4 in. modularity principle and leave the resulting jointing in the capable hands of the bricklayer. Depending on the *actual* dimensions of the brick, the mason will adjust the mortar joint, usually within a range between ⅜ in. and ½ in., to achieve the 4 in. module. It may take as many as five courses to achieve a multiple of 4 in., as with the engineer modular size and the engineer Norman size, or just a single course as with the utility size.

Table 5.2 indicates the quantities of modular face brick that are required to construct 1,000 sq ft of single-wythe wall and the number of courses required to achieve a multiple of 4 in. Table 5.3 provides designers and estimators with coursing heights using a range of modular brick sizes.

Table 5.2 A Guide to Estimating Brick Quantities in Walls.

Designation Unit	Nominal Dimensions (in.) W x H x L	Quantity of Face Brick Required to Construct 1,000 sq ft*	Modular Coursing
Modular, Stretcher Face	4 × 2⅔ × 8	6,750	3 courses = 8 in.
Modular, Shiner Face	4 × 2⅔ × 8	4,500	1 course = 4 in.
Engineer Modular	4 × 3⅕ × 8	5,625	5 courses = 16 in.
Closure Modular	4 × 4 × 8	4,500	1 course = 4 in.
Roman	4 × 2 × 12	6,000	2 courses = 4 in.
Norman	4 × 2⅔ × 12	4,500	3 courses = 8 in.
Engineer Norman	4 × 3⅕ × 12	3,750	5 courses = 16 in.
Utility	4 × 4 × 12	3,000	1 course = 4 in.

*Quantities based on a running bond pattern. Credit: Brick Industry Association

Table 5.3 Vertical Coursing, with Brick Positioned as Stretchers or Headers. "C" = courses. Credit: Brick Industry Assoc.

No. Of Courses	Vertical Coursing of Unit			
	2C = 4 in.	*3C = 8 in.*	*5C = 16 in.*	*1C = 4 in.*
1	0' 2"	0' 2⅔"	0' 3⅕"	0' 4"
2	0' 4"	0' 5⅓"	0' 6⅖"	0' 8"
3	0' 6"	0' 8"	0' 9⅗"	1' 0"
4	0' 8"	0' 10⅔"	1' 0⅘"	1' 4"
5	0' 10"	1' 1⅓"	1' 4"	1' 8"
6	1' 0"	1' 4"	1' 7⅕"	2' 0"
7	1' 2"	1' 6⅔"	1' 10⅖"	2' 4"
8	1' 4"	1' 9⅓"	2' 1⅗"	2' 8"
9	1' 6"	2' 0"	2' 4⅘"	3' 0"
10	1' 8"	2' 2⅔"	2' 8"	3' 4"
11	1' 10"	2' 5⅓"	2' 11⅕"	3' 8"
12	2' 0"	2' 8"	3' 2⅖"	4' 0"
13	2' 2"	2' 10⅔"	3' 5⅗"	4' 4"
14	2' 4"	3' 1⅓"	3' 8⅘"	4' 8"
15	2' 6"	3' 4"	4' 0"	5' 0"
16	2' 8"	3' 6⅔"	4' 3⅕"	5' 4"
17	2' 10"	3' 9⅓"	4' 6⅖"	5' 8"
18	3' 0"	4' 0"	4' 9⅗"	6' 0"
19	3' 2"	4' 2⅔"	5' 0⅘"	6' 4"
20	3' 4"	4' 5⅓"	5' 4"	6' 8"
21	3' 6"	4' 8"	5' 7⅕"	7' 0"
22	3' 8"	4' 10⅔"	6' 1⅗"	7' 4"
23	3' 10"	5' 1⅓"	6' 4⅘"	7' 8"
24	4' 0"	5' 4"	6' 8"	8' 0"

A vital design tool for designers working with brick and block is a set of brick scales. Brick scales provide accurate templates for both visual layout and numerical dimensioning of brick and block courses. This information is provided for both vertical and horizontal coursing and is given at a variety of standard architectural drawing scales. Brick scales not only facilitate the

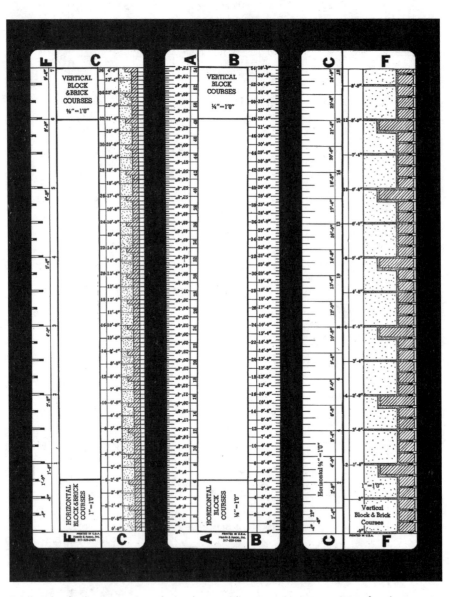

Brick scales facilitate masonry design by providing coursing at a variety of scales.

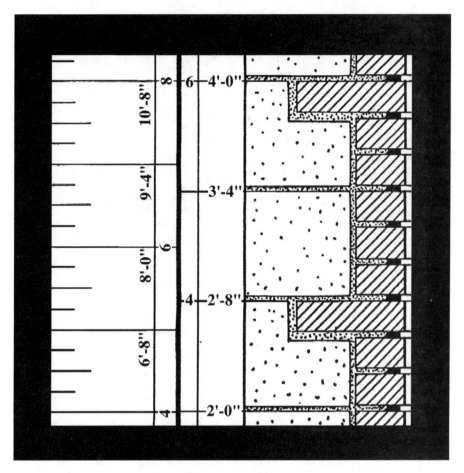

Precise modular coursing is provided, eliminating the need for time-consuming calculations.

design process, but guarantee greater accuracy with less waste and result in fewer costly on-site cuts.

The number of bricks that require cutting within a particular wall bond or paving pattern will impact both the total quantity of bricks and the cost of installation. Cutting is typically required at the ends or corners of walls, where closer bricks or bats are needed, and at the edges of brick pavements. Project masons can often recommend minor changes that dramatically reduce the number of cuts required for installation. Using the 4 in. modular grid and employing brick scales as a design tool will help minimize the need for excessive cutting.

THE BUSY DESIGNER'S QUICK REFERENCE GUIDE:
Estimating Brick Quantities

- In both design and layout, estimating is facilitated by the modularity of brick.

- Actual joint widths will be established by the bricklayer to achieve modularity in coursing.

- Modular bricks achieve a vertical multiple of 4 in. in one to five courses, depending on unit height.

- Brick scales facilitate both design and estimating, and are available in a range of standard architectural scales, from ⅛" = 1' 0" to 1½" = 1' 0".

APPENDIX  A

METRIC STANDARDS FOR BRICK MASONRY

Public law has identified the metric system as the preferred system of weights and measures for trade and commerce in the United States. Given the variations of metric systems currently in place throughout the world, the French *système international d'unités* (SI) has been adopted for implementation in the United States. The use of millimeters as been adopted by most major codes. The utilization of such a small basic increment has led to the virtual elimination of the decimal point. Although this is quite convenient for brick and mortar, it has resulted in some awkwardly long measurements in other trades.

METRIC MODULARITY

Whereas the inch-pound system of masonry modularity bases its nominal dimensions on multiples or fractions of 4 in., the basic module of the SI metric system is 100 mm. (This is conveniently close to 4 in., which converts to 101.6 mm.) Using millimeters eliminates fractions and yields full integers for dimensioning, but at the expense of a certain degree of rounding off.

In the case of masonry, metric conversion seems to offer some significant design advantages. The *specified* width, height, and length of a "metric modular brick" are 90 mm, 57 mm, and 190 mm respectively. This would equate to a brick that is 3⁹⁄₁₆ in. by 2¼ in. by 7½ in. Earlier we identified a modular brick as having specified dimensions of 3⅝ by 2¼ by 7⅝ when a ⅜ in. mortar joint is used, or dimensions of 3½ by 2¼ by 7½ when a ½ in. joint is used. Thus, the metric modular brick falls neatly into this range. The *nominal* dimensions of the same brick are 100 mm by 67 mm by 200 mm. The advantages of such even round numbers in two of the three nominal dimensions becomes immediately apparent. In the SI system, a 10 mm joint is typically used (this is slightly larger than ⅜ in.). Three courses of 57 mm bricks, plus three 10 mm mortar joints totals 201 mm. This is rounded off to 200 mm, a convenient increment for designers to work with. Because this is quite close to the 8 in. (or 203.2 mm) achieved by three modular courses, it will facilitate conversion to metric by American designers and the brick industry. As with all brick, the actual (manufactured) dimension will vary slightly from the specified dimension. These differences are simply made up in the field and can be disregarded by designers, provided they adhere to the principle of modularity. Table A.1 provides metric standards for height, coursing, and length of bricks.

Table A.1 Nominal and Coordinating Metric Dimensions for Brick.

Nominal Height (mm)	Modular Coursing	Coordinating Length (mm)
50	2 courses = 100 mm	300
67	3 courses = 200 mm	200
		300
75	4 courses = 300 mm	200
		300
80	5 courses = 400 mm	200
		300
100	1 course = 100 mm	200
		300
		400
133	3 courses = 400 mm	200
		300
		400
150	2 courses = 300 mm	300
		400
200	1 course = 200 mm	200
		300
		400
300	1 course = 300 mm	300

Several manufacturers can currently produce brick in metric sizes, although it probably means a special order for most. Designers should anticipate the generally longer lead time and extra costs associated with specifying metric units.

APPENDIX B

TECHNICAL RESOURCES FOR DESIGNERS

Fortunately, there are a growing number of resources whose primary mission is to assist designers and specifiers with questions regarding masonry detailing and practices. Manufacturers and suppliers remain a good source of reliable data, although this information has the potential of being proprietary in nature. Regional and national organizations not directly tied to the manufacturing, supplying, or sales of brick are also excellent sources of information. The recent explosion of Internet-based information, coupled with its ease of availability, has tremendously facilitated the accessing of design-related information, and most organizations now offer a wide range of technical information via the web.

An impressive depth and diversity of brick-related technical information is available via the Worldwide Web.

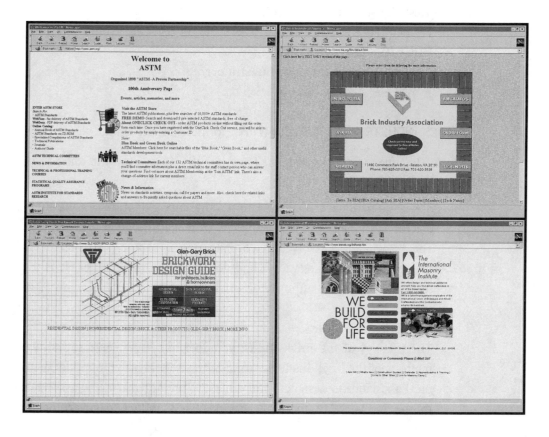

ORGANIZATIONS

American Society for Testing and Materials (ASTM)

The ASTM establishes and publishes approved guides, practices, and test methods for a wide range of industry materials. Topics range from construction materials to amusement rides to nuclear energy. Standards are available in both book and CD-ROM formats, and available on the Internet. The ASTM also sponsors technical and professional training programs, as well as continuing research programs. The ASTM states that its fundamental mission is "to be the foremost developer and provider of voluntary consensus standards, related technical information, and services having internationally recognized quality and applicability that: promote public health and safety, and the overall quality of life; contribute to the reliability of materials, products, systems and services; and facilitate national, regional, and international commerce."

> **American Society for Testing and Materials**
> 100 Barr Harbor Drive
> West Conshohocken, PA 19428
> Phone: 610-832-9500
> Fax: 610-832-9555
> Internet Address: **http://www.astm.org/**
> E-mail: **service@astm.org**

Brick Industry Association (BIA) (formerly Brick Institute of America)

In its document *Introduction to the Brick Industry Association*, the role of BIA is neatly defined.

> BIA is the national trade association representing distributors and manufacturers of clay brick and suppliers of related products and services. The Association is involved in a broad range of technical, research, marketing, government relations, and communications activities. It is the recognized national authority on brick construction.

> *BIA's Mission*
> The mission of the Brick Industry Association is to serve the united interests of the brick manufacturing industry, primarily: to render technical assistance to designers and others; to provide marketing assistance to the industry; to monitor and positively influence governmental

actions; to assure the long-term availability of bricklayers; and to provide other member services, as appropriate. BIA's programs are designed to accomplish objectives which either cannot be achieved by the members themselves, or are more efficiently carried out collectively.

It is difficult to imagine a masonry-related article, book, or publication that does not cite BIA's *Technical Notes* as a primary source of information. Its continuing efforts to disseminate reliable technical information on masonry design have led to the development of a CD-ROM version of *Technical Notes* and, more recently, a user-friendly web site containing useful technical design data and links. The Brick Industry Association is also responsible for the color periodical *Brick in Architecture*, which occasionally features site-related installations. The significant contributions made by BIA have earned it the unofficial title "The National Authority on Brick Construction."

Brick Industry Association
11490 Commerce Park Drive
Reston, VA 20191
Phone: 703-620-0010
Fax: 703-620-3928
Internet Address: **http://www.brickinfo.org/**

CONSTRUCTION SPECIFICATIONS INSTITUTE (CSI)

CSI describes itself as "a national professional association that provides technical information and products, continuing education, professional conferences, and product shows to enhance communication among all the non-residential building design and construction industry's disciplines and meet the industry's need for a common system of organizing and presenting construction documents." As its title implies, the CSI focuses on (but is not limited to) the preparation and organization of technical specifications for the design and construction trades.

Construction Specifications Institute
601 Madison Street
Alexandria, VA 22314-1791
Phone: 800-689-2900 or 703-684-0300
Fax: 703-684-0465
Internet Address: **http://www.csinet.org/**

INTERNATIONAL MASONRY INSTITUTE (IMI)

In its promotional material IMI states, "IMI offers design and technical assistance and will help you find skilled craftworkers in all of the trowel trades. IMI is a labor/management cooperative of the International Union of Bricklayers and Allied Craftworkers and the Contractors who employ its members." The Institute sponsors an impressive number of educational programs, targeted toward craftsworkers, engineers, and designers. Its annual National Masonry Camp brings masons, architects, and landscape architects together for an intensive week-long program intended to educate and to bridge the gap that too often exists between designers and masons. Other sponsored programs include the annual Boiler Brick Bowl at Purdue University and the Exploration in Masonry program at the University of Notre Dame, along with numerous other university programs across the

IMI sponsors a variety of educational programs, including Purdue University's annual "Boiler Brick Bowl." Design students are teamed with bricklayers to gain insight into the construction site.

United States. The Institute's free Lunchbox Seminars series specifically targets designers, engineers, and construction managers, addressing their masonry-related questions. In addition, IMI hosts the annual Golden Trowel Awards program, recognizing excellence in masonry design.

Of particular value to designers are IMI's multivolume set of Masonry Bibliographies. These contain a comprehensive list of masonry-related publications. IMI will answer technical questions over the phone or via its Internet site.

International Masonry Institute

James Brice House
42 East Street
Annapolis, MD 21401
1-800-IMI-0988
Internet Address: **http://www.imiweb.org/**

IMI also maintains regional and area offices across the country, which provide assistance with design and engineering questions. They are listed in the regional index that follows this section.

THE MASONRY SOCIETY (TMS)

TMS describes its organization thus:

> The Masonry Society is an international gathering of people interested in the art and science of masonry. It is a professional, technical, and educational association dedicated to the advancement of knowledge on masonry. TMS members are design engineers, architects, builders, researchers, educators, building officials, material suppliers, manufacturers, and others who want to contribute to and benefit from the global pool of knowledge on masonry.

> TMS gathers and disseminates technical information through its committees, publications, codes and standards, slide sets, videotapes, computer software, newsletter, refereed journal, educational programs, professors' workshop, scholarships, certification programs, disaster investigation team, and conferences.

Among the many activities of The Masonry Society is its Disaster Investigation Team, a unit that seeks to determine specific causes of masonry failure resulting from natural and human-caused catastrophic events and to formulate methods of future mitigation.

The Masonry Society

3970 Broadway, Suite 201-D
Boulder, CO 80304-1135
Phone: 303-939-9700
Fax: 303-541-9215
Internet Address: **http://www.masonrysociety.org/**

MASONRY CONTRACTORS ASSOCIATION OF AMERICA (MCAA)

The Masonry Contractor's Association of America exists, as its name implies, as a service organization primarily serving masonry contractors. MCAA is actively involved in education, training, research, promotion, and safety, related to the use of masonry products in the construction trade. It also serves its members by maintaining an active presence in Washington, D.C., where the MCAA endeavors to assist and monitor construction-related legislation and regulation.

Masonry Contractors Association of America

1910 S. Highland Avenue, Suite 101
Lombard, IL 60148
Phone: 1-800-536-2225 or 630-705-4200
Fax: 630-705-4209
Internet Address: **http://www.masoncontractors.com/**

NATIONAL CONCRETE MASONRY ASSOCIATION (NCMA)

On its web site, the NCMA describes its role as follows.

The National Concrete Masonry Association, established in1918, is the national trade association representing the concrete masonry industry. The Association is involved in a broad range of technical, research, marketing, government relations and communications activities. NCMA is an association of producers of concrete masonry products, and suppliers of products and services related to the industry. NCMA offers a variety of technical services and design aids through publications, computer programs, slide presentations and technical training.

NCMA's Mission:

The NCMA defines its mission as follows:

National Concrete Masonry Association's Mission is to advance, support and serve the common interests of its members as well as to enhance their position as industry leaders and innovators through the manufacturing, marketing and application of concrete masonry and related products and systems that are affordable, technically sound, and environmentally safe, and to meet the future needs of the market.

The Association also offers a number of training programs and product testing certification courses as components in its education programs. Of special interest to landscape designers may be NCMA's Block and Landscape Products Sales School. Among other topics of study, it covers "an overview of concrete masonry systems, segmental retaining walls and interlocking concrete pavers."

National Concrete Masonry Association
2302 Horse Pen Road
Herndon, VA 20171
Phone: 703-713-1900
Internet address: **http://www.ncma.org/**

REGIONAL ASSOCIATIONS

Most states or regions have local associations that not only offer technical assistance, but because of their geographical proximity, can often provide on-site evaluation and consultation. Typically, their role is to promote sound (and frequent) use of masonry in local construction projects, and they can serve as a valuable technical and practical resource during the design phase of a project. Consult your local chapter of the International Union of Bricklayers and Allied Craftworkers for the masonry industry association nearest you. Although their addresses and telephone numbers change too frequently for inclusion here, a list is provided for reference purposes.

Alabama Masonry Institute
Arizona Masonry Guild Inc.
Brick Association of the Carolinas
Brick Distributors of Wisconsin

Brick Institute of America—Mid-East Region

Brick Institute of California

Delaware Valley Masonry Institute

Illinois Masonry Institute, Masonry Advisory Council

International Masonry Institute

International Masonry Institute, New England Masonry Center

International Masonry Institute, Great Lakes Masonry Center

International Masonry Institute, Market Development Headquarters

International Masonry Institute, Michigan Area Office

International Masonry Institute, Minnesota Area Office

International Masonry Institute, New Jersey Masonry Training Center

International Masonry Institute, New York City Office

International Masonry Institute, New York State Office

International Masonry Institute, Ohio Area Office

Kansas Masonry Industries Council

Kentuckiana Masonry Institute

Masonry and Ceramic Tile Institute of Oregon

Masonry Association of Florida Inc.

Masonry Council of Canada

Masonry Institute (Northern California)

Masonry Institute of America

Masonry Institute of British Columbia

Masonry Institute of Columbus

Masonry Institute of Dayton

Masonry Institute of Fresno

Masonry Institute of Iowa

Masonry Institute of Michigan

Masonry Institute of Southern Illinois

Masonry Institute of St. Louis

Masonry Institute of Tennessee

Masonry Institute of Texas

Masonry Institute of Washington

Masonry Resource of Southern California

Mississippi-Louisiana Brick Manufacturers Association

Nebraska Masonry Institute

Rocky Mountain Masonry Institute

Southern Brick Institute

Southwestern Brick Institute

The Masonry Institute, Inc.

Western States Clay Products Association

COMPUTER AIDS

Listings that qualify in this category will undoubtedly grow, but there are currently a handful of computer-based design resources:

ARCH. Analyzes the performance of brick arches. Available from the Brick Industry Association.

CAVWAL. Assists in the design of nonbearing cavity walls. Available from the National Concrete Masonry Association.

Masonry Compute. A computational aid available from the International Masonry Institute.

MASRET. Aids and evaluates the design of masonry retaining walls. Available from the National Concrete Masonry Association.

Electronic Technical Notes on Brick Construction. Contains the entire Technical Notes series in CD-ROM format. Available from the Brick Industry Association.

APPENDIX  C

A GLOSSARY OF BRICK TERMS

Glossary is reproduced with the permission of the Brick Industry Association (* indicates definitions provided by the author).

Absorption: The weight of water a brick unit absorbs when immersed in either cold or boiling water for a stated length of time. Expressed as a percentage of the weight of the dry unit. See ASTM Specification C67.

Admixtures: Materials added to mortar to impart special properties to the mortar.

Anchor: A piece or assemblage, usually metal, used to attach building parts (e.g., plates, joists, trusses, etc.) to masonry or masonry materials.

ANSI: American National Standards Institute.

Arch: A curved compressive structural member spanning openings or recesses; also built flat.

Back arch: A concealed arch carrying the backing of a wall where the exterior facing is carried by a lintel.

Jack arch: An arch having horizontal or nearly horizontal upper and lower surfaces. Also called *flat* or *straight* arch.

Major arch: An arch with spans greater than 6 ft and equivalent to uniform loads greater than 1,000 lb per ft. Typically known as a Tudor arch, semicircular arch, Gothic arch, or parabolic arch. Has a rise to span ratio greater than 0.15.

Minor arch: An arch with maximum span of 6 ft and loads not exceeding 1,000 lb. per ft. Typically known as a jack arch, segmental arch, or multicentered arch. Has a rise to span ratio less than or equal to 0.15.

Relieving arch: An arch built over a lintel, flat arch, or smaller arch to divert loads, thus relieving the lower member from excessive loading. Also known as a *discharging* or *safety arch*.

155

Trimmer arch: Usually a low-rise arch of brick, used for supporting a fireplace hearth.

Ashlar masonry: Masonry composed of rectangular units of burned clay or shale, or stone, generally larger in size than brick and properly bonded, having sawed, dressed, or squared beds, and joints laid in mortar. Often the unit size varies to provide a random pattern, *random ashlar.*

ASTM: American Society for Testing and Materials.

Backfilling: 1. Rough masonry built behind a facing or between two faces. 2. Filling over the extrados of an arch. 3. Brickwork in spaces between structural timbers, sometimes called *brick nogging.*

Backup: That part of a masonry wall behind the exterior facing.

Bat: A piece of brick.

Batter: A recessed or sloped masonry surface achieved in successive courses; the opposite of corbel.

Bed joint: The horizontal layer of mortar on which a masonry unit is laid.

Belt course: A narrow horizontal course of masonry, sometimes slightly projected, such as windowsills that are made continuous. Sometimes called *string course* or *sill course.*

Blocking: A method of bonding two adjoining or intersecting walls, not built at the same time, by means of offsets whose vertical dimensions are not less than 8 in.

Bond: 1. Tying various parts of a masonry wall by lapping units one over another or by connecting with metal ties. 2. Pattern formed by exposed faces of units. 3. Adhesion between mortar or grout and masonry units or reinforcement.

Bond beam: Course or courses of a masonry wall grouted and usually reinforced in the horizontal direction. Serves as a horizontal tie for a wall, a bearing course for structural members, or as a flexural member itself.

Bond course: A course consisting of units that overlap more than one wythe of masonry.

Bonder: A bonding unit. See *header.*

Breaking joints: Any arrangement of masonry units that prevents continuous vertical joints from occurring in adjacent courses.

Brick: A solid masonry unit of clay or shale, formed into a rectangular prism while plastic, and burned or fired in a kiln.

Acid-resistant brick: Brick suitable for use in contact with chemicals, usually in conjunction with acid-resistant mortars.

Adobe brick: Large, roughly molded, sun-dried clay brick of varying size.

Angle brick: Any brick shaped to an oblique angle to fit a salient corner.

Arch brick: Wedge-shaped brick for special use in an arch.

Building brick: Brick for building purposes not especially treated for texture or color. Formerly called *common brick.* See ASTM Specification C62.

Clinker brick: A very hard-burned brick whose shape is distorted or bloated owing to nearly complete vitrification.

Common brick: See *building brick.*

Dry-press brick: Brick formed in molds under high pressures from relatively dry clay (5% to 7% moisture content).

Economy brick: Brick whose nominal dimensions are 4 × 4 × 8 in.

Engineered brick: Brick whose nominal dimensions are 4 × 3.2 × 8 in.

Facing brick: Brick made especially for facing purposes, often treated to produce surface texture. Such bricks are made of selected clays, or treated, to produce desired color. See ASTM Specification C216.

Fire brick: Brick made of refractory ceramic material that will resist high temperatures.

Floor brick: Smooth, dense brick, highly resistant to abrasion, used as finished floor surfaces. See ASTM Specification C410.

Gauged brick: 1. Brick that has been ground or otherwise produced to accurate dimensions. 2. A tapered arch brick.

Hollow brick: A masonry unit of clay or shale whose net cross-sectional area in any plane parallel to the bearing surface is not less than 60% of its gross cross-sectional area measured in the same plane. See ASTM Specification C652.

Jumbo brick: A generic term indicating a brick larger in size than the standard. Some producers use this term to describe oversize brick of specific dimensions that they manufactured.

Norman brick: A brick whose nominal dimensions are 4 × 2⅔ × 12 in.

Paving brick: Vitrified brick especially suitable for use in pavements where resistance to abrasion is important. See ASTM Specification C902 or C1272.

Roman brick: Brick whose nominal dimensions are 4 × 2 × 12 in.

Salmon brick: Generic term for underburned bricks that are more porous, slightly larger, and lighter colored than hard-burned brick. Usually pinkish orange color.

Sewer brick: Low-absorption, abrasive-resistant brick intended for use in drainage structures. See ASTM Specification C32.

Soft-mud brick: Brick produced by molding relatively wet clay (20% to 30% moisture). Often a hand process. When insides of molds are sanded to prevent sticking of clay, the product is *sand-struck* brick. When molds are wetted to prevent sticking, the product is *water-struck* brick.

Stiff-mud brick: Brick produced by extruding a stiff but plastic clay (12% to 15% moisture) through a die.

Brick and brick: A method of laying brick so that units touch each other, with only enough mortar to fill surface irregularities.

Brick grade: Designation for durability of a unit, expressed as SW for severe weathering, MW for moderate weathering, or NW for negligible weathering. See ASTM Specifications C216, C62, and C652.

Brick type: Designation for facing brick that controls tolerance, chippage, and distortion. Expressed as FBS, FBX, and FBA for solid brick, and HBS, HBX, HBA, and HBB for hollow brick. See ASTM Specifications C216 and C652.

Buttering: Placing mortar on a masonry unit with a trowel.

C/B ratio: The ratio of the weight of water absorbed by a masonry unit during immersion in cold water to weight absorbed during immersion in boiling water. An indication of the probable resistance of brick to freezing and thawing. Also called *saturation coefficient*. See ASTM Specification C67.

Centering: Temporary formwork for the support of masonry arches or lintels during construction. Also called *center(s)*.

Ceramic color glaze: An opaque colored glaze of satin or gloss finish obtained by spraying the clay body with a compound of metallic oxides, chemicals, and other clays. A unit is burned at high temperatures, fusing glaze to body to make them inseparable. See ASTM Specification C126.

Chase: A continuous recess built into a wall to receive pipes, ducts, etc.

Clay: A natural mineral aggregate consisting essentially of hydrous aluminum silicate; it is plastic when sufficiently wetted, rigid when dried, and vitrified when fired to a sufficiently high temperature.

Clay-mortar mix: Finely ground clay used as a plasticizer for masonry mortars.

Clear ceramic glaze: Same as *ceramic color glaze,* except that it is translucent or slightly tinted, with a gloss finish.

Clip: A portion of a brick cut to length.

Clipped header: A brick, usually a half-bat, cut to simulate a header in appearance.

Closer brick: The last masonry unit laid in a course. It may be a whole unit or a portion of a unit.

Closure brick: Supplementary or short-length units used at corners or jambs to maintain bond patterns.

Collar joint: The vertical, longitudinal joint between wythes of masonry.

Column: A vertical member whose horizontal dimension measured at right angles to the thickness does not exceed three times its thickness.

Coping: The material or masonry units forming a cap or finish on top of a wall, pier, pilaster, chimney, etc. It protects masonry below from penetration of water from above.

Corbel: A shelf or ledge formed by projecting successive courses of masonry out from the face of a wall.

Course: One of the continuous horizontal layers of units, bonded with mortar in masonry.

Culls: Masonry units that do not meet standards or specifications and have been rejected.

Damp course: A course or layer of impervious material that prevents capillary entrance of moisture from the ground or a lower course. Often called *damp check*.

Dampproofing: Prevention of moisture penetration by capillary action.

*Diaper: A visual pattern, usually diamond-shaped, in a vertical brick surface. The pattern often results from augmenting a specific bond through the use of brick of contrasting colors and/or finishes.

Dog's tooth: Brick laid with its corners projecting from the wall face.

Drip: A projecting piece of material, shaped to throw off water and prevent its running down the face of a wall or other surface.

Effective height: The height of a member to be assumed for calculating the slenderness ratio.

Effective thickness: The thickness of a member to be assumed for calculating the slenderness ratio.

Effloresence: A powder or stain sometimes found on the surface of masonry, resulting from deposition of water-soluble salts.

Engineered brick masonry: Masonry in which design is based on a rational structural analysis.

Face: 1. The exposed surface of a wall or masonry unit. 2. The surface of a unit designed to be exposed in the finished masonry.

Facing: Any material, forming a part of a wall, used as a finished surface.

Field: The expanse of wall between openings, corners, etc., principally composed of stretchers.

Fire clay: A clay that is highly resistant to heat without deforming and is used for making brick.

Fireproofing: Any material or combination of materials protecting structural members to increase their fire resistance.

Fire-resistive material: See *noncombustible material.*

Flashing: 1. A thin impervious material placed in mortar joints and through air spaces in masonry to prevent water penetration and/or provide water drainage. 2. Manufacturing method to produce specific color tones.

Frog: A depression in the bed surface of a brick. Sometimes called a *panel.*

Furring: A method of finishing the interior face of a masonry wall to provide space for insulation, prevent moisture transmittance, or provide a level surface for finishing.

Grounds: Nailing strips placed in masonry walls as a means of attaching trim or furring.

Grout: Mixture of cementitious material and aggregate to which sufficient water is added to produce pouring consistency without segregation of the constituents.

High-lift grouting: The technique of grouting masonry in lifts up to 12 ft.

Low-lift grouting: The technique of grouting as the wall is constructed.

Hacking: 1. The procedure of stacking brick in a kiln or on a kiln car. 2. Laying brick with the bottom edge set in from the plane surface of the wall.

Hard-burned: Nearly vitrified clay products that have been fired at high temperatures. They have relatively low absorptions and high compressive strengths.

Head joint: The vertical mortar joint between ends of masonry units. Often called a *cross joint.*

Header: A masonry unit that overlaps two or more adjacent wythes of masonry to tie them together. Often called a *bonder.*

Blind header: A concealed brick header in the interior of a wall, not showing on the face.

Clipped header: A bat placed to look like a header for purposes of establishing a pattern. Also called a *false header.*

Flare header: A header of darker color than the field of the wall.

Heading course: A continuous bonding course of header brick. Also called a *header course.*

Initial rate of absorption: The weight of water absorbed expressed in g per 30 sq in. of contact surface when a brick is partially immersed for one minute. Also called *suction.* See ASTM Specification C67.

IRA: See *initial rate of absorption.*

Kiln: A furnace oven or heated enclosure used for burning or firing brick or other clay material.

Kiln run: Bricks from one kiln that have not been sorted or graded for size or color variation.

King closer: A brick cut diagonally to have one 2 in. end and one full-width end.

Lateral support: Means whereby walls are braced either vertically or horizontally by columns, pilasters, cross walls, beams, floors, roofs, etc.

Lead: The section of a wall built up and racked back on successive courses. A line is attached to leads as a guide for constructing a wall between them.

Lime, hydrated: Quicklime to which sufficient water has been added to convert the oxides to hydroxides.

Lime putty: Hydrated lime in plastic form ready for addition to mortar.

Lintel: A beam placed over an opening in a wall.

Masonry: Brick, stone, concrete, etc., or masonry combinations thereof, bonded with mortar.

Masonry cement: A mill-mixed cementitious material to which sand and water must be added. See ASTM C91.

Masonry unit: Natural or manufactured building units of burned clay, concrete, stone, glass, gypsum, etc.

Hollow masonry unit: A unit whose net cross-sectional area in any plane parallel to the bearing surface is less than 75% of the gross.

Modular masonry unit: A unit whose nominal dimensions are based on the 4 in. module.

Solid masonry unit: A unit whose net cross-sectional area in every plane parallel to the bearing surface is 75% or more of the gross.

Mortar: A plastic mixture of cementitious materials, fine aggregate, and water. See ASTM Specifications C270, C476 or the Brick Industry Association's (BIA) M1-72.

Fat mortar: Mortar containing a high percentage of cementitious components. This is a sticky mortar that adheres to a trowel.

High-bond mortar: Mortar that develops higher bond strengths with masonry units than normally developed with conventional mortar.

Lean mortar: Mortar that is deficient in cementitious components; it is usually harsh and difficult to spread.

Nominal dimension: A dimension greater than a specified masonry dimension by the thickness of a mortar joint, but not more than ½ in.

Noncombustible material: Any material that will neither ignite nor actively support combustion in air at a temperature of 1,200°F (649°C) when exposed to fire.

Overhand work: Laying brick from inside a wall, by workers standing on a floor or on a scaffold.

Pargeting: The process of applying a coat of cement mortar to masonry. Often spelled and/or pronounced *parging*.

Partition: An interior wall, one story or less in height.

Pick and dip: A method of laying brick whereby the bricklayer simultaneously picks up a brick with one hand and, with the other hand, enough mortar on a trowel to lay the brick. Sometimes called the *Eastern* or *New England* method.

Pier: An isolated column of masonry.

Pilaster: A wall portion projecting from either or both wall faces and serving as a vertical column and/or beam.

Plumb rule: A combination plumb rule and level, used in a horizontal position as a level and in a vertical position as a plumb rule. This tool is made in lengths of 42 in. and 48 in., and in short lengths from 12 in. to 24 in.

Pointing: Troweling mortar into a joint after masonry units are laid.

Prefabricated brick masonry: Masonry construction fabricated in a location other than its final in-service location in a structure. Also known as *preassembled, panelized,* and *sectionalized* brick masonry.

Prism: A small masonry assemblage made with masonry units and mortar. Primarily used to predict the strength of full-scale masonry members.

Queen closer: A cut brick having a nominal 2 in. horizontal face dimension.

Quoin: A projecting right-angle masonry corner.

Racking: A method entailing stepping back successive courses of masonry.

Raggle: A groove in a joint or special unit to receive roofing or flashing.

RBM: Reinforced brick masonry.

Reinforced masonry: Masonry units, reinforcing steel, and grout and/or mortar combined to act together in resisting forces.

Return: Any surface turned back from the face of a principal surface.

Reveal: That portion of a jamb or recess that is visible from the face of a wall.

Rowlock: A brick laid on its face edge so that the normal bedding area is visible in the wall face. Frequently spelled *rolok*.

Salt glaze: A gloss finish obtained by thermochemical reaction between silicates of clay and vapors of salt or chemicals.

Saturation coefficient: See *C/B ratio.*

Shale: Clay that has been subjected to high pressures until it has hardened.

Shoved joint: Vertical joint filled by shoving a brick against the next brick when it is being laid in a bed of mortar.

*Skintle: A technique of laying brick wherein one corner of the exposed face is angled outward from the flush vertical surface of the surrounding wall. Skintling is most commonly random, but may also be used to develop geometric patterns.

Slenderness ratio: Ratio of the effective height of a member to its effective thickness.

Slushed joint: Vertical joint filled, after units are laid, by "throwing" mortar in with the edge of a trowel. (Generally not recommended.)

Soap: A masonry unit of normal face dimensions, having a nominal 2 in. thickness.

Soffit: The underside of a beam, lintel, or arch.

Soft-burned: Clay products that have been fired at low temperature ranges, producing relatively high absorptions and low compressive strengths.

Solar screen: A perforated wall used as a sunshade.

Soldier: A stretcher set on end with its face showing on the wall surface.

Spall: A small fragment removed from the face of a masonry unit by a blow or by action of the elements.

Stack: Any structure or part thereof that contains a flue or flues for the discharge of gases.

Story pole: A marked pole for measuring masonry coursing during construction.

Stretcher: A masonry unit laid with its greatest dimension horizontal and its face parallel to the wall face.

Stringing mortar: The procedure of spreading enough mortar on a bed to lay several masonry units.

Struck joint: Any mortar joint that has been finished with a trowel.

Suction: See *initial rate of absorption*.

Temper: To moisten and mix clay, plaster, or mortar to a proper consistency.

Tie: Any unit of material that connects masonry to masonry or other materials. See *wall tie*.

Tooling: Compressing and shaping the face of a mortar joint with a special tool other than a trowel.

Toothing: Constructing the temporary end of a wall with the end stretcher of every alternate course projecting. Projecting units are *toothers*.

Traditional masonry: Masonry in which design is based on empirical rules that control minimum thickness, lateral support requirements, and height without a structural analysis.

Tuck pointing: The filling in with fresh mortar of cut-out or defective mortar joints in masonry.

Veneer: A single wythe of masonry for facing purposes, not structurally bonded.

Virtual eccentricity: The eccentricity of a resultant axial load required to produce axial and bending stresses equivalent to those produced by applied axial loads and moments. It is normally found by dividing the moment at a section by the summation of axial loads occurring at that section.

Vitrification: The condition resulting when kiln temperatures are sufficient to fuse grains and close pores of a clay product, making the mass impervious.

Wall: A vertical member of a structure whose horizontal dimension measured at right angles to the thickness exceeds three times its thickness.

Apron wall: That part of a panel wall between a windowsill and wall support.

Area wall: 1. The masonry surrounding or partly surrounding an area. 2. The retaining wall around basement windows below grade.

Bearing wall: A wall that supports a vertical load in addition to its own weight.

Cavity wall: A wall built of masonry units so arranged as to provide a continuous air space within the wall (with or without insulating material), and in which the inner and outer wythes of the wall are tied together with metal ties.

Composite wall: A multiple-wythe wall in which at least one of the wythes is dissimilar to the other wythe or wythes in respect to the type or grade of masonry unit or mortar.

Curtain wall: An exterior non-load-bearing wall not wholly supported at each story. Such walls may be anchored to columns, spandrel beams, floors, or bearing walls, but not necessarily built between structural elements.

Dwarf wall: A wall or partition that does not extend to the ceiling.

Enclosure wall: An exterior nonbearing wall in skeleton frame construction. Such walls are anchored to columns, piers, or floors, but not necessarily built between columns or piers nor wholly supported at each story.

Exterior wall: Any outside wall or vertical enclosure of a building other than a party wall.

Faced wall: A composite wall in which the masonry facing and backing are so bonded as to exert a common reaction under load.

Fire division wall: Any wall that subdivides a building so as to resist the spread of fire. It is not necessarily continuous through all stories to and above the roof.

Fire wall: Any wall that subdivides a building to resist the spread of fire and that extends continuously from the foundation through the roof.

Foundation wall: That portion of a load-bearing wall below the level of the adjacent grade, or below first-floor beams or joists.

Hollow wall: A wall built of masonry units arranged to provide an air space within the wall. The separated facing and backing are bonded together with masonry units.

Load-bearing wall: A wall that supports any vertical load in addition to its own weight.

Non-load-bearing wall: A wall that supports no vertical load other than its own weight.

Panel wall: An exterior, non-load-bearing wall wholly supported at each story.

Parapet wall: That part of any wall entirely above the roof line.

Party wall: A wall used for joint service by adjoining buildings.

Perforated wall: A wall that contains a considerable number of relatively small openings. Often called a *pierced wall* or a *screen wall.*

Shear wall: A wall that resists horizontal forces applied in the plane of the wall.

Single-wythe wall: A wall containing only one masonry unit in wall thickness.

Solid masonry wall: A wall built of solid masonry units, laid contiguously, with joints between units completely filled with mortar or grout.

Spandrel wall: That part of a curtain wall above the top of a window in one story and below the sill of the window in the story above.

Veneered wall: A wall having a facing of masonry units or other weather-resisting noncombustible materials securely attached to the backing, but not so bonded as to intentionally exert common action under load.

Wall plate: A horizontal member anchored to a masonry wall to which other structural elements may be attached. Also called *head plate.*

Wall tie: A bonder or metal piece that connects wythes of masonry to each other or to other materials.

Wall tie, cavity: A rigid, corrosion-resistant metal tie that bonds two wythes of a cavity wall. It is usually steel, 3/16 in. in diameter, and formed in a **Z** shape or a rectangle.

Wall tie, veneer: A strip or piece of metal used to tie a facing veneer to the backing.

Water retentivity: That property of a mortar that prevents the rapid loss of water to masonry units of high suction. It prevents bleeding or water gain when mortar is in contact with relatively impervious units.

Water table: A projection of lower masonry on the outside of a wall slightly above the ground. Often a damp course is placed at the level of the water table to prevent upward penetration of groundwater.

Waterproofing: Prevention of moisture flow through masonry caused by water pressure.

Weep holes: Openings placed in mortar joints of facing material at the level of flashing, to permit the escape of moisture.

With inspection: Masonry designed with the higher stresses allowed under engineered brick masonry (EBM). Requires the establishment of procedures on the job to control mortar mix, workmanship, and protection of masonry materials.

Without inspection: Masonry designed with the reduced stresses allowed under EBM.

Wythe: 1. Each continuous vertical section of masonry one unit in thickness. 2. The thickness of masonry separating flues in a chimney. Also called *withe* or *tier.*

BIBLIOGRAPHY

Beall, Christine. "Hiding Exposed Flashings." *Masonry Construction* (Jan. 1990): 25.

———. "Installing Weep Holes." *Masonry Construction* (April 1991): 138–139.

———. *Masonry Design and Detailing*. 3d ed. McGraw Hill, New York, 1993.

———. "Residential Screen Walls." *Masonry Construction* (Aug. 1990): 380–382.

———. "Masonry Buildings and Environmental Concerns." *Masonry Construction* (Apr. 1994): 162–166.

Borchelt, J. Gregg. "How Brick Sculpture Is Made." *Masonry Construction* (May 1991): 180–184.

Brick Institute of America (now Brick Industry Association). *Technical Notes on Brick Construction*. BIA, Reston, VA.

Brick Industry Association. *Electronic Technical Notes on Brick Construction*, Version 1.0. BIA, Reston, VA, 1996.

Brickwork in Italy, A Brief Review from Ancient to Modern Times. American Face Brick Association, Chicago, 1925.

Camillo, Jim. "How Bricks Are Made." *Masonry Construction* (Aug. 1993): 354–359.

Carroll, John. "Designing Residential Brick Flatwork." *Masonry Construction* (Nov. 1994): 506–510.

Clifton, James R., ed. *Cleaning Stone and Masonry*. ASTM Special Technical Publication 935, 1986.

Curtis, Paul G. "Connecting Brick to Backups." *Masonry Construction* (June 1990): 248–250.

Drysdale, G., A. A. Hamid, and L. R. Baker. *Masonry Structures, Behavior and Design*. Prentice-Hall, Englewood Cliffs, NJ, 1994.

Harrison, Peter J. *Brick Pavement*. The Dietz Press, Richmond, VA, 1994.

Hooker, Kenneth. "Building Quoins." *Masonry Construction* (Jan. 1993): 17–18.

————. "Building Serpentine Walls." *Masonry Construction* (May 1993): 204–205.

————. "Reducing Efflorescence Potential." *Masonry Construction* (Feb. 1994): 76–79.

————. "Masonry Materials and Environmental Concerns." *Masonry Construction* (Apr. 1994): 167–171.

————. "Designing and Building Pilasters." *Masonry Construction* (May 1995): 214–218.

————. "Computing Aids for Masonry Structural Design." *Masonry Construction* (Mar. 1996): 125–129.

Jewell, Linda. "Perforated Brick Walls." *Landscape Architecture* (May/June 1983): 88–90.

Keating, Elizabeth. "Brick Sculpture Scores." *Masonry Construction* (Apr. 1997): 186–190.

Kicklighter, Clois E. *Modern Masonry, Brick, Block, Stone*. Goodheart-Willcox South Holland, IL, 1991.

Koski, John A. "Removing Efflorescence." *Masonry Construction* (May 1992): 174–177.

Laska, Walter. "Detailing Brick Corbeling." *Masonry Construction* (Dec. 1991): 478–479.

————. "Proper Drainage for Weep Holes." *Masonry Construction* (Aug. 1992): 313–317.

Lilley, Alan. A. *A Handbook of Segmental Paving*. Van Nostrand Reinhold, New York, 1991.

Lloyd, Nathaniel. *A History of English Brickwork*. H. Greville Montgomery, London, 1925. Reprint, Antique Collector's Club Ltd., 1983.

London, Mark. *Masonry, Respectful Rehabilitation: How to Care for Old and Historic Brick and Stone*. National Trust for Historic Preservation. The Preservation Press, Washington, D.C., 1988.

Lynch, Gerard C. J. *Gauged Brickwork: A Technical Handbook*. Gower Technical Press, Aldershot, UK, 1990.

Marshall, Nancy J. "Clinker Brick: Overfired Brick Can Add Texture to a Masonry Wall." *Masonry Construction* (Jan. 1990): 32–34.

Mulligan, John A. *Handbook of Brick Masonry Construction*. McGraw-Hill Book Company, New York, London, 1942.

1991 Masonry Codes and Specifications, with 1992 Supplements. Masonry Promotion Groups of Southern California, 1992.

Nunn, Mark A. "Exterior Brick Pavements." *The Construction Specifier* (Sept. 1989): 101–107.

Perlman, Paul H. "Choosing Brick for Curved Walls." *Masonry Construction* (Mar. 1992): 103–105.

———. "Using Soldier Courses Properly." *Masonry Construction* (July 1992): 245–247.

Plummer, Harry C. *Brick and Tile Engineering Handbook of Design.* Structural Clay Products Institute, McLean, VA, 1955.

Plumridge, Andrew, and William Meulenkamp, *Brickwork: Architecture and Design.* Harry N. Abrams, New York, 1993.

Ramsey, Charles G., and Harold R. Sleeper. *Architectural Graphic Standards,* 9th ed. John Wiley & Sons, New York, 1994.

Santilli, Chris. "Pretty Patterns." *Masonry Construction* (Jan. 1991): 14–16.

Seakins, L. W., and S. Smith. *Practical Brickwork.* Chemical Publishing Company, New York, 1963.

Sorvig, Kim. "Earth Building in Landscape Architecture." *Landscape Architecture* (Feb. 1995): 28–32.

Stoddard, Ralph P. *Brick Structures: How to Build Them.* McGraw-Hill Book Company, New York, 1946.

Trimble, Brian E. "Back to Brick." *Landscape Architecture* (Dec. 1996): 32–37.

Walker, Theodore. *Site Design and Construction Detailing.* PDA Publishers, West Lafayette, IN, 1978.

Wallace, Mark A. "Pavers Prosper." *Masonry Construction* (May 1990): 214–216.

Hanson, Richard E. Jr., and Angelo Simeoni. *ASLA Handbook of Landscape Architectural Construction,* vol. 4, "Materials." Weinberg-Coyle, ed. LAF, Washington, D.C., 1992. Chapter 4.

Winterbottom, Daniel. "Baked Earth." *Landscape Architecture* (May 1989): 102–106.

———. "Sculpted Brick." *Landscape Architecture* (Nov. 1990): 76–77.

———. "Sculpted Brick II." *Landscape Architecture* (Dec. 1990): 62–64.

Frank Lloyd Wright: Writings and Buildings. Selected by Edgar Kaufmann and Ben Raeburn, eds. Meridian Books, New York, 1960.

Selected Technical Notes on Brick Construction, Brick Industry Association

Brick Floors and Pavements, Parts I, II, and III, 14, 14A, 14B

Salvaged Brick, 15

Design and Detailing of Movement Joints, 18A

Brick in Landscape Architecture, Pedestrian Applications, 29

Brick in Landscape Architecture, Garden Walls, 29A

Brick in Landscape Architecture, Miscellaneous Applications, 29B

Bonds and Patterns in Brickwork, 30

Brick Masonry Details, Caps and Copings, Corbels and Racking, 36A

Testing for Engineered Brick Masonry Brick, Mortar and Grout, 39

Wall Ties for Brick Masonry, 44B

Other Technical Guidelines

Exterior Paving With Brick, Glen-Gery Brickwork Techniques.

Water Permeance of Masonry Walls, Glen-Gery Brickwork Techniques.

Grimm, C. T. *Cleaning Masonry: A Review of the Literature.*

———. *Water Permeance of Masonry Walls: A Review of the Literature.*

Burchelt, J. G., ed. *Masonry: Materials, Properties and Performance*, ASTM STP 778 (ASTM, 1982), 178–199.

Good Practice for Construction of Mortarless Brick Paving and Flooring, Brick Association of North Carolina.

Flexible Brick Pavements: Heavy Vehicular Pavements, Design and Installation Guide, Brick Industry Association, 1991.

Flexible Brick Pavements: Pedestrian and Light Vehicular Traffic Application, Brick Industry Association, 1992.

INDEX